KUNDA

A MODERN VIEW

KUNDALINI
A MODERN VIEW

Darrel Irving

JAICO PUBLISHING HOUSE

Mumbai Delhi Bangalore Kolkata
Hyderabad Chennai Ahmedabad Bhopal

Published by Jaico Publishing House
121 Mahatma Gandhi Road
Mumbai - 400 001
jaicopub@vsnl.com
www.jaicobooks.com

Published in arrangement with
Darrel Irving
255 West 91st St. Apt. 1-B
New York, NY 10024
U.S.A.

KUNDALINI: A MODERN VIEW
ISBN 81-7224-758-3

First Jaico Impression: 1999
Fifth Jaico Impression: 2006

Printed by
New Radharaman Printers
20, Wadala Udyog Bhavan
Wadala, Mumbai-400 031

This book is about kundalini, one of the most splendid and mysterious of known phenomena. Those who have experienced it describe it as a light flaring up in the darkness, a supernatural power, magical and beguiling, sometimes fierce and terrible, yet marvelous, and always awesome in its manifestation. You may ask just who are those who know of this wonder, since most people have no knowledge of it, especially if you yourself have never heard this word before. But in reality, kundalini is as familiar as your own fingers reaching to turn this page; it is as tangible as the vision with which your eyes peruse these sentences; and it is as comprehensible as the thoughts forming in your mind in response to these words. For kundalini is the very force and thrust of life—it is the life force itself.

CONTENTS

CONTENTS

ACKNOWLEDGMENTS

Though there were many factors that led to the inception, development, and completion of this book, the most memorable was the generosity of friends, colleagues, and associates who gave voluntarily of their time and help whenever I asked it of them. Their insight and understanding often lit the way ahead for me, and their thoughtful advice and counsel were indispensible in bringing this book to fruition. I would like, therefore, to express my gratitude:

To Susan Tredway, who responded to my initial and tentative curiosity about kundalini with the gift of Ajit Mookerjee's book, *Kundalini, The Arousal of the Inner Energy.*

To Mary Ann Wrobleski, who has always been supportive of my literary efforts, and, even more importantly, of spiritual values, and who introduced me to Gene Kieffer.

To Gene Kieffer, scholar, mythologist, and fount of information, who was always able to provide answers to my questions about kundalini, not only in an historical and mythological context, but with erudition and discernment as well.

To my brother David, for just being there, for his significant editorial contribution, and for his steadfast and never failing support.

To Joy Smith, editor and writer, who is uniquely gifted at articulating the most subtle nuances of thought, whose editorial comments were invaluable, and whose review of my manuscript gave me the confidence that my book was ready to send out into the world.

To Michel Méry, avant-garde fellow writer, who has been supportive of this text and who is representative of a new attitude in science extending beyond prevailing mechanistic scientific credos and theories.

To Carolla Burroughs, for her insightful suggestions on the first draft of my kundalini experience and for encouraging me to continue with my text.

To Ming Yen Tung for her computer illustration of the Sahasrara chakra from Arthur Avalon's *The Serpent Power*.

To Michelle McKee, librarian at the Kristine Mann Library of the C. G. Jung Center in New York City, for her kindness and courtesy and who, because of her comprehensive grasp of Jungian source materials, was able to guide me to the precise information I required.

To my agent, John White, for believing in my book, and for helping overcome the considerable obstacles to placing a book with a publisher.

To the entire staff at Weiser Publishing, Inc., for their efforts on behalf of my manuscript; to Donald Weiser, publisher, for his commitment to producing spiritual books.

INTRODUCTION
The Mystery of the Serpent

"Science, whose soul is explanation, halts with hostile front when faced with mystery." From our point of view, these words by George Eliot ought to be engraved on the walls of every institution dedicated to the understanding of the mind. For not only was George Eliot a writer of formidable intelligence, she was also a novelist blessed with sufficient inventive power to create the Reverend Edward Casubon, a fictional character so unique that his driving life's ambition was to publish a "Key to All Mythologies."[1]

If alive today, more than a century later, it is conceivable that Eliot would have convinced the Reverend Casaubon, a "man of profound learning," that Kundalini holds the key not only to *the* mysteries, but to the mysteries of the mind as well, and would have set him to the task of working on a book very much in sympathy with *Serpent of Fire*.

In some quarters it was not long ago that the Serpent of Fire was not acknowledged as even existing. I can recall an incident that took place when I gave a lecture on Kundalini at a university in New York State. Just as I finished my introduction, there was a commotion in the first row directly in front of the podium. A white-haired gentleman had begun to fidget, then wave a hand in the air and mumble something that sounded like, "No, no, you're all wrong. There's no such thing!" Moments later, he stalked out of the auditorium with a small cluster of students in his wake. I learned afterwards that the man was a distinguished professor of Oriental religions. It seemed that his magnum opus, a study of the world's

---

[1] *Middlemarch* by George Eliot (New York: Penguin Books, 1994), p. 63.

religions, had just recently come off the press, and although it marked the culmination of a lifetime of research, it contained not a single mention of kundalini, i.e., the Serpent of Fire.

At that moment, this omission must have been quite an embarrassment to him, with so many of his students in attendance at that lecture. And it is curious that when compiling his book he ignored one of the oldest and most dominant strains of spiritual and religious thought. One would have thought that he would have at least perused *The Serpent Power*, by Sir John Woodruff, and two or three books on the Tantras, if only in passing. In the years since then, however, I have seen again and again that it is entirely possible for a scholar to devote an entire professional life to the study of the world's religions and still remain in the dark about Kundalini, so elusive has this mysterious entity remained down through the centuries. Some scholars, on the other hand, do not shrink from the facts before them. Plenty of Joseph Campbell's students, could, for instance, testify that when it comes to mythology, there are signs of Kundalini to be found almost everywhere. Campbell was profoundly interested in Kundalini, in fact, and an entire chapter of *Serpent of Fire* is devoted to Campbell's fascination with this subject. There are other serious investigators, too, with minds receptive to "new" ideas. C. G. Jung, for instance, was keenly interested in Kundalini and wrote a paper titled "The Realities of Practical Psychotherapy,"[2] in which he connected the Kundalini *chakras* with psychogenic disturbances. He is cited in this text for a seminar he held in 1932 on the chakra symbolism of Tantric Yoga, particularly on the ideas and images of the Kundalini system.

---

[2]The notes of Mary Foote in her introduction to Lectures I and II, by C. G. Jung, in *Spring* 1975, an Annual of Archetypal Psychology and Jungian Thought, New York, pp. 1–2. See also page 144 of this text.

Although Jung linked the Serpent Power with the unconscious—a debatable point at best—that is not an issue here. What matters is that he was sufficiently knowledgeable about Kundalini to try to integrate it with his own way of thinking about the mind and with his particular system of symbolism.

"It is as if the Kundalini in its movement upwards were pulling us up with it," he writes, "as if I were part of that movement, particularly in the beginning. It is true that we *are* a part, because we are then that which contains the Gods. They are germs in us, germs in the *muladhara* [the root chakra at the base of the spine], and when that upheaval comes, we are carried with it, and naturally we might think we were moving upwards. . . . So it is wise not to identify with these experiences, but to handle them as if they were outside the human realm. That is the safest thing to do—and really absolutely necessary. Otherwise, as I said, you get an inflation, and inflation is just a minor form of lunacy, a mitigated term for it. And if you get so absolutely inflated that you burst, it is schizophrenia.

"Therefore the Yoga way or the Yoga philosophy has always been a secret, but not because people have *kept* it secret. For as soon as you keep a secret, it is already an open secret: you know about it and other people know about it, and then it is no longer a secret. The real secrets are secrets because nobody understands them. One cannot even talk about them, and of such a kind are the experiences of the Kundalini Yoga."[3]

This was undoubtedly true when written more than sixty years ago. But much has been said about Kundalini since then, and personal experiences are being reported frequently today. The difficulty is that it is rare to find any-

---

[3]Lecture II, by C. G. Jung, in *Spring* 1975, An Annual of Archetypal Psychology and Jungian Thought, New York, pp. 19–20.

one who can even begin to do justice to such experiences with words. One exception is the author of this book, *Serpent of Fire*, as the reader will shortly discover.

So far as we know, Sigmund Freud did not mention Kundalini in his writings, but his contributions to psychology were so great that the oversight can be considered of little consequence. What should bother us, however, is the current failure on the part of today's leading lights in the field of psychology, who apparently feel their understanding of mental illness, and of the human potential, is sufficient unto itself and requires no further insights. What hundreds of ancient adepts had to say about the mind and how it works seems not to matter to them at all. For the sake of reducing hostilities, however, perhaps we should try to concur with Freud's admonishment: "Do not judge too harshly of a first attempt at picturing a thing so elusive as the human mind. The deeper we probe in our study of mental processes, the more we become aware of the richness and complexity of their content."[4]

So recently has modern psychology been founded that it was little more than a century ago that people, including doctors, believed mental disease was caused by evil spirits. The practice of exorcism, in fact, is still practiced by some clergymen today, though rarely. Psychoses, however, are as old as the hills. A British psychiatrist has written that contrary to the popular belief that madness has been with us for the past 10,000 years, it has actually been around for more than twenty-five times that long. "A known and historical act of madness by Homo sapiens occurred a quarter of a million years ago, and that was when they annihilated the Neanderthal man."[5]

[4]*New Introductory Lectures on Psychoanalysis* by Sigmund Freud (New York: W. W. Norton & Company, 1933), p. 110.
[5]*The Origin of Madness*, by Dr. M. E. Elsarrag, consultant psychiatrist to Whitchurch and Ely Hospitals (Cardiff, Wales: C S Printing of Cardiff), p. 5.

Schizophrenia, once known as *dementia praecox*, is the most common of the serious mental problems and is said to account for almost half of the mental hospital population in most of the industrialized countries. It is a splitting of the personality or breaking away from reality, and its main symptom is emotional abnormality, generally tending toward apathy. The first to draw parallels between processes in schizophrenia and mythology was, of course, C. G. Jung. Although thousands of other psychologists have followed his lead, discovering for themselves the same kinds of correlations he did, their interpretations may not hold up to scrutiny in the years to come. Because so long as the Reverend Casubon's "Key to All Mythologies" remains only a novelist's fantasy, such parallels constitute little more than the faint glimmer of a future science. The real question with regard to such corollaries should be concerned with what the mythmakers actually had in mind when they invented their mythologies. The archetypes *are* embedded in the psyche, yes, but how they got there in the first place is a question even more compelling and that has yet to be answered in a convincing way.

M. Esther Harding, a disciple of Jung, points out that the difference between what is normal and what is abnormal is largely a matter of degree. "When a modern individual becomes alienated, as Jonah obviously did," she says, "there is little that friends or even the physician can do to help. He can perhaps suggest the attitude that will bring the patient back into relation with his inner voice; for the rest he can merely watch the stages of the regression, hoping that the sufferer will hear the inner voice in time to allow of his return to the world. . . ."[6]

---

[6]*Psychic Energy, Its Source and Goal*, by M. Esther Harding. Bollingen Series X (New York: Pantheon Books, 1947), p. 278.

xvi ■ Darrel Irving

Freud did not draw a sharp line between the concepts of normal and neurotic, either. One of the key statements in his writings was the dictum that "we are all somewhat hysterical." In other words, we all have an inner voice that speaks to us at various times and in different ways, and the difference between sanity and madness is the manner and intensity with which that voice expresses itself. For Harding, it is "an invasion of strange and dynamic material from the unconscious."[7]

However similar two different brains may appear on the surface, that "dynamic material" within the cells can range from the sublime to the chaotic. For the mystic, there may be inner scenes of heavenly beauty and the sounds of celestial music. But for the psychotic, the same brain cells may pour out the tormenting shrieks and unbearable sights of hell.

Except where a pathological condition exists, the cause responsible for either extreme is unknown. Can anyone explain how a Titian, Michelangelo, Mozart, or Beethoven creates a masterpiece? Or how a physicist like Einstein arrives at a new vision of the cosmos? Take the not-so-extraordinary case of the 18th century mathematical prodigy Carl Friedrich Gauss. At age 9, he entered the reckoning class at the town school in Braunschweig, Germany, where he was born. The teacher gave out a complex numerical series to be added. Scarcely had the teacher finished speaking when Gauss threw his slate on the table, as was the custom, exclaiming, "There it lies!" The other scholars, all much older than Gauss, continued their figuring. When the slates were examined at the end of the hour, Gauss had only one number on his slate, the correct result.

---

[7]*Psychic Energy, Its Source and Goal*, by M. Esther Harding. Bollingen Series X (New York: Pantheon Books, 1947), p. 279.

This was commonplace for Gauss, whose power of mental calculation was unsurpassed. He could carry on difficult and extensive numerical investigations with incredible ease.[8]

The only rational theory that could explain the diverse and baffling mental phenomena exhibited by the human brain would have to presume the existence of an intelligent nerve energy, or life energy. If so, this would provide the first comprehensive, unifying principle that could illuminate the stage on which the greatest dramas of all are enacted from moment to moment in all our lives—the mind.

It is a sad fact that, for the most part, priests, yogis, and metaphysicians of the last few thousand years have known little or nothing about this life energy. Those who were knowledgeable called it *prana, chi,* or by many other names. For, though known to few in general, this life energy was, nevertheless, known in many different places, and Jung, in fact, compiled some fifty names for it in his writings. Christopher Hills, author of more than a dozen books on yoga and human evolution says this very same energy "is the link to knowing the nuclear center of the Self, for without some way of reading the intelligence of the Tao and mapping the path of kundalini through the spiritual vehicle, mankind is just as ignorant of himself as the day he was born."[9]

Gopi Krishna, who was instrumental in introducing Kundalini to the West in his autobiography[10] more than a

---

[8]*The Unfathomed Mind: A Handbook of Unusual Mental Phenomena,* by William R. Corliss (Glen Arm, MD: The Sourcebook Project, 1982), p. 325.
[9]*The Rise of the Phoenix* by Christopher Hills (Boulder Creek, CA: Common Ownership Press, 1979), p. 382.
[10]*Kundalini, the Evolutionary Energy in Man,* by Gopi Krishna (Boston: Shambhala, 1967, 1970).

quarter century ago, says, "Prana is immaterial, invisible and imperceptive to our senses. But it has influence over the molecules, atoms and even sub-atomic particles. In its most concentrated form, it is present in the human reproductive system, the seed containing the most concentrated form of all. Why some brains are more intelligent than others depends on the *prana* or, more precisely, the spectrum of the *prana*. . . . [When this pranic spectrum changes] for whatever reason, the concentrated prana in the reproductive organs goes into the spinal cord and flows upward into the brain.[11] This process is called the awakening of kundalini.

Kundalini, then, is the mechanism at the base of the spine that controls the production and quality of prana, or the life energy. When the awakening occurs, it is as though a chemical factory is opened in the body; the more powerful reproductive *prana* begins to circulate throughout the nervous system and brain, regulating the activity of the organs and causing them to function in a more efficient, healthy way. If the organs and blood are unhealthy, that will affect the quality of the *prana* circulating in the brain, causing mental disease in all its varied forms.

Why modern psychology has not already begun empirical research on prana is another of the great twentieth century mysteries. The current attitude of science toward what is held to be mysterious by laymen—UFO's, out-of-body experiences, mysticism, and other strange or abnormal phenomena, mental or otherwise—is perhaps sufficient explanation. We should be reminded, however, that even major scientific theories have had to be over-

---

[11]Gopi Krishna, in a conversation with Yvonne Kason, M.D., in New York, NY, 1978. From *Interviews with Gopi Krishna* (Darien, CT: Kundalini Research Foundation, Ltd.; and Toronto: F.I.N.D. Research, 1991), p. 184.

hauled or scrapped altogether from time to time in order to accommodate new observations.

One wonders, could the general antipathy of science toward Kundalini be rooted in gender? The Serpent Power has always been addressed in the feminine—as a Goddess—in nearly all of the sacred texts of antiquity. Or could it simply be because we instinctively know what havoc can occur in the mind if this Goddess is heedlessly awakened from her slumber at the base of the spine?

Distinctly aware of this danger, Lilian Silburn begins her book, *Kundalini—The Energy of the Depths*, with a stern warning: "The mysterious energy aroused by Kundalini yoga manifests with a violence beyond belief and cannot be manipulated without incurring certain risks. (Some deviations are termed 'demonic,' as they lead to depression and insanity.) Therefore, to probe into her secrets, one must seek the help of a master belonging to a special lineage and endowed with unfailing knowledge. It cannot be over-emphasized that without such a guide, or by following a powerless and ignorant teacher, the arousal of Kundalini will have disastrous results."[12]

This admonition, coming from a scientist who has earned worldwide respect as Director of Research at the National Scientific Research Institute in Paris and who is a leader in the studies of Kashmiri Shaivism, flies in the face of what a good many of today's "masters of Kundalini yoga" say when they are recruiting new students. One notes that many of these modern-day teachers, those who can find no mystery in Kundalini and who, therefore, are able to advertise themselves (in good conscience) as masters of the ancient science, would be hard-pressed to write a single, original para-

---

[12]*Kundalini—The Energy of the Depths* by Lilian Silburn (Albany: State University of New York Press, 1988), p. xiii.

graph describing it. Dr. Silburn's statement also makes one wonder about the efficacy of what thousands of Americans are experiencing when they receive *shaktipat* (transmission of bioenergy, or prana, through the guru's touch, words, look, or thoughts) from their favorite gurus. It is well to bear in mind with regard to such teaching, therefore, that insofar as the Goddess Kundalini is concerned, all, even scholars and those with the most impressive credentials, are mere novitiates when faced with the mystery of the Serpent.

Mention of Kashmiri Shaivism serves as a reminder that the Indian state of Kashmir was once the heartland of the Sacred Science of Kundalini. Not very long ago the adventurous tourist, with ample time and resolve, could find there more than 800 temples and shrines devoted to the Goddess. It should not be surprising then to learn that the Himalayan foothills surrounding Dal Lake, in the Vale of Kashmir, was once home to generations of *rishis*, or enlightened seers, men and women whose literary productions were unsurpassed for their insights into *the Reality*. The following stanzas from *Secrets of Kundalini in Panchastavi*, an extraordinary hymn to Kundalini written a thousand years ago by an anonymous sage, were randomly chosen from the hundred and forty-six that comprise the book:[13]

> O Mother: He who contemplates Thee, even for an instant, like the fine fibre stretching out from the juice of the lac, that devotee of noble virtues becomes the object of undivided attention, in the abode of Cupid, on the part of the youthful maidens tormented by love.

---

[13]*Secrets of Kundalini in Panchastavi*, by Gopi Krishna (New Delhi: Kundalini Research & Publication Trust, 1978), pp. 213, 232, 233.

O Mother: Those who meditate on thee as the purifier of the six paths, blazing like millions of destructive fires, and flooding these worlds with the torrential rain of nectar, as also a maiden in full youth with bulging breasts, Thou bring them fullness, and they thus become world-teachers.

O Mother: some (of Thy devotees) call Thee as Supreme Knowledge, some as the encompassing atmosphere, some as (the Font of) bliss and some as Maya (veil of illusion), while others see Thee as the Universe and still others in the form of a Guru (who is) limitless compassion personified.

O Thou Mother of all the worlds, why speak further (about Thy attributes)? Our only prayer is (that) Thou may manifest Thyself to us in Thy supreme dark-blue aspect, like a host of blue water-lilies with curly, moist, glistening, tawny hair and with protruding breasts hanging down on Thy beautiful waist.

O Mother of the Universe. Thou shinest as the moon to dispel the darkness, dread and fever of embodied life. All these followers of different creeds, in the dark about Thy real nature, disputing with each other, stumbling and sinking deeper into the web of Thy illusion, helpless to save themselves, go to destruction. But we (Thy devotees), bowing to Thee, seek Thy protection, O Sovereign of the worlds.

Here, in these lines of poetry, is enough mystery to last a lifetime. One of the most prominent and endearing appellations bestowed upon Kundalini was to call her "Vak, the Goddess of Speech." With lines such as these, one can begin to appreciate the power of the poet.

It is a pity that Nobel Prize scientist Francis Crick could not have been similarly inspired by the Goddess Vak before writing a recent magazine article titled "Science, Soul, and the Astonishing Hypothesis." In the article, Crick poses a rhetorical question: "Is there some soul, or spirit, that science cannot explain, without which we would not be conscious and which survives our physical death?" He then answers his own question like this: "Many people believe that there must be, because they cannot see how the activity of nerve cells can possibly explain what philosophers call 'qualia'; for example, the painfulness of pain or the redness of red. What I have called the Astonishing Hypothesis says, on the contrary, that it's all due to the activities of nerve cells (and associated cells and molecules). This idea—that it's all in the brain—is not new; it goes back at least as far as Hippocrates, who lived around 400 B.C."[14]

In other words, Dr. Crick is saying that the brain is something like a television broadcasting station and a TV set all in one, e.g., it both transmits the program and receives it at the same time. From this it would follow that mental illnesses like schizophrenia will, in time, be amenable to cure by purely chemical or surgical means; that with a little more knowledge, we should be able to produce crops of geniuses almost at will because, after all, it's all in the brain cells.

Can it really be that simple? A quick reading of *Secrets of Kundalini in Panchastavi*, or any of a hundred other ancient esoteric texts would speak to the contrary. Dr. Crick is correct about one thing, however, when he

---

[14]"The Astonishing Hypothesis," in *Skeptical Inquirer Magazine*, Committee for the Scientific Investigation of Claims of the Paranormal (Amherst, NY), January/February 1995, pp. 37–38.

says, "There is no reason why we should not start the study of consciousness experimentally and press on relentlessly until we have uncovered all the intricate mechanisms involved."[15] But he is incorrect when he finds a place for *all* of these mechanisms within the brain itself.

The author of the tenth book of the *Rig Veda* (the oldest, or one of the oldest sacred texts of the Hindus) would agree. Addressing Kundalini as Vak, he has the Goddess say, "I make the man I love exceeding mighty, make him a sage, a rishi, and a Brahman." This is another way of saying that Kundalini can transform an ordinary man or woman into a world teacher. It is absolutely inconceivable that any chemical, no matter how subtle or complex science can make it, even in the ages to come, will be able to transform an ordinary man or woman into a genius. That is something reserved for the Goddess Kundalini alone.

Almost as astonishing as Dr. Crick's hypothesis was an article by Dr. Carl Sagan, appearing in the same issue of the magazine. In it, the prolific popularizer of science admits to having had rather frequent hallucinations. He writes, "I have, maybe a dozen times since my parents died, heard one of them say my name; just the single word, 'Carl.' I miss them; they called me by my first name so much during the time they *were* alive; I was in the practice of responding instantly when I was called; it has deep psychic roots. So my brain plays it back every now and then. This doesn't surprise me at all; I sort of like it. But it's a hallucination. If I *were* a little less skeptical, though, I could see how easy it

---

[15]"The Astonishing Hypothesis," in *Skeptical Inquirer Magazine*, January/February 1995, pp. 37–38.

would be to say, 'They're around somewhere. I can hear them.' "[16]

This is rather typical of how scientists respond to mysteries they are unable to solve. They simply call the mystery a hallucination and say it is all in the brain. Yet, there may be hope for them. Though they may be obstinate when it comes to accepting that there do exist intelligent forces of nature that are hidden at present, many of the most talented among them, like Sagan, waver on the edge of the mystical state, needing only a nudge to fall into the unfathomable world of the Illuminate. "And the word was made flesh and dwelt among us . . . full of grace and truth" (John, I, 14).

David Bohm, the theoretical physicist, raises the question: How do we understand the processes that govern a world wherein the old analytic categories of subject and object must break down, and where what is left is something ultimately beyond words or numbers? His answer was to give the underlying, outerlying, or higher unseen reality a name, the *Implicate Order*. This would be the place for containing all that was latent or nonmanifest.[17]

The theoretical physicists of antiquity, seeking to identify and name that same unseen Reality, would call it the Goddess of Illusion, or Kundalini. Is the answer to this issue, then, only a matter of semantics? Shall we just pass it off by saying, a rose by any other name would smell as sweet? Or is it something altogether different? Many writers who have backgrounds in physics don't

---

[16]"Wonder and Skepticism," in *Skeptical Inquirer Magazine*, January/February 1995, p. 29.
[17]*The Sphinx and the Rainbow*, by David Loye (Boston: Shambhala, 1983), p. 151.

seem to think so. They see the world of the physicist and the mystic as essentially identical, because, as they say, "all is One, and that One is nothing at all." This is surely not a very satisfying, nor a satisfactory explanation.

From what we have learned in talking to hundreds of individuals who have been diagnosed as having one form of mental illness or another, it does make a difference. As the author of this book makes clear, if a psychosis is caused by Kundalini, simply knowing it is so can have a very beneficial effect, one that is almost instantaneous, provided the word Kundalini is correctly defined.

That is the reason *Serpent of Fire* could greatly help restore hope, health, and happiness to hundreds, or thousands, even millions, of individuals who are suffering from schizophrenia. This is a rare book, indeed, for here we have an author who has skillfully combined thorough research with deep insight and personal experience into a convincing case in favor of the argument that schizophrenia is the Serpent of Fire known from immemorial times as Kundalini.

Once those who are afflicted with the agonizing maladies of mental illness become aware of the facts so artfully presented here, their gloomy, chaotic, and terrifying picture of the world should almost certainly begin to make sense and brighten; for such is the power of truth.

The author has carefully examined the evidence and concluded that the mysterious force—the Serpent of Fire—not only lurks behind schizophrenia but also has the power to cleanse, heal, rejuvenate, and restore the psyche as well, if given half a chance.

All too often, however, persons diagnosed as schizophrenic are doused with Thorazine, Stelazine, Lithium, or "a host of other chemicals designed to slay the kundalini serpent in its tracks." That is precisely why this book is so timely and important. The accepted methods of treatment are not working. Today's mental institutions cannot begin to accommodate the number of patients requiring help.

The implications inherent in what the author has laid before us are so enormous as to be almost unimaginable. They go far beyond what we can see with our naked eyes. Yes, knowledge of the Serpent of Fire can work miracles in the wards of our mental hospitals—and in the lives of those suffering from mental illness—but it could do a great deal more. As the author makes abundantly clear, this knowledge would point the way to greatly expanded consciousness for thousands of men and women everywhere, and it would be those Enlightened souls who lead the world into the Golden Age that is about to dawn.

—Gene Kieffer

Chapter 1

Why
Kundalini?

Kundalini is one of the most fascinating, yet most perplexing of Eastern ideas. Other metaphysical topics, such as Tao, Zen, channeling, rolfing, astral travel, reincarnation, psychometry, gems, stones, crystals, Sufism, Edgar Cayce readings, biofeedback, Transcendental Meditation, and Yoga, are widely discussed and generally understood. Absent from this tableau for the most part, however, are discussions about kundalini. There are a few accounts: Gopi Krishna's *Kundalini, The Evolutionary Energy in Man*[1] most notably; some scholarly works, such as Sir John Woodroffe's *The Serpent Power*,[2] Mary Scott's *Kundalini in the Physical World*;[3] or the informative *Kundalini: The Arousal of the Inner Energy* by Ajit Mookerjee;[4] and numerous treatises by Gene Kieffer, one of the leaders in the kundalini movement. But most new age writers and gurus have steered clear of this theme simply because it remains an enigma to them. Thus, the kundalini literature remains scant and as little is known today as in preceding generations.

I became curious about kundalini as the result of a mystical experience that prompted me to explore the subject of enlightenment. (This is fully discussed in chapter 3.) My interest led me to various religious and/or philosophical disciplines such as Zen, Yoga, Buddhism, Tao, Gurdjieff, Ouspensky, and eventually to the writings and lectures of the religious thinker, Jiddu Krishnamurti. In Krishnamurti I found the answers I was looking for. His approach was intelligent and objective. He emphasized the "real," the "what is"; nothing was to be taken upon faith, and he abhorred the role of guru. The titles of Krishnamurti's books and talks are indicative of his essential teachings: *Thought Breeds Fear, Freedom from the Known, Education and the Significance of Life, Mind in Meditation, This Light in Oneself, The Awakening of Intelligence.*[5] Krishnamurti seemed to be a truly enlightened man. He rejected all ideas, thoughts, words, or gestures that betokened any kind of belief system or mystical conjecture. He urged his listeners to be choicelessly aware, moment to moment, of the movement of the mind, both at the superficial and at the deeper levels. In this kind of attention, he informed them, there existed the possibility of transformation.

I studied Krishnamurti's ideas for a number of years, searching to discover within myself the transformation he called upon his audiences to find. Eventually I read the biographies of Krishnamurti's life written by Mary Lutyens, *Krishnamurti: The Years of Awakening* and *Krishnamurti: The Years of Fulfillment,*[6] and the biography titled *Krishnamurti* by Pupul Jayakar.[7] Both authors were more than just associates of Krishnamurti, they were his close friends and were themselves deeply committed to understanding his thought. I discovered that each author had detailed the events and moments surrounding Krishnamurti's actual illumination. This had occurred when he was a young man of 28 years. To my utter amazement, both accounts described a profound kundalini experience. This was disconcerting news. For every word Krishnamurti had uttered for some sixty years had inherently rejected any and all occurrences of an occult nature. And kundalini must surely be considered among the most esoteric of occult phenomena. I subsequently wrote to one of the biographers, Pupul Jayakar, and inquired if she knew why Krishnamurti had directed the focus of his teaching away from the kundalini that appeared to be the very source of his own spiritual awakening. Mrs. Jayakar replied that she herself had tried to discuss this with Krishnamurti but that he had little memory of what had taken place. In fact, Mrs. Jayakar described a long group discussion with some of Krishnamurti's old friends present, where he had inquired whether anyone could refresh his memory as to what had happened with regard to this question. This was in the early 1980s when Krishnamurti was already past 80. She further informed me that Krishnamurti had not been interested in probing these past events. For he had felt strongly that focusing on the circumstances of his own psychic experiences or pursuing extrasensory mysteries would not lead to any expansion of the human brain. Such an expansion could be achieved only through an attention, a seeing, a listening and learning which erased the grooves of psychological memory in the human brain. This of course, is the very essence of Krishnamurti's message.

Be that as it may, from both biographer's accounts, it seemed apparent, nevertheless, that the means by which Krishnamurti himself had become released from the bonds of psychological memory was nothing less than that of activated kundalini energy. I began to investigate kundalini and started to learn of other individuals, including Gopi Krishna, who will be discussed in detail in this text, in whom kundalini had been directly connected to occurrences of heightened self-realization. Additionally, it was becoming clear that my own mystical experience, which had brought me to this quest in the first place, also fit snugly within the kundalini parameters. Gradually I came to realize that kundalini, although mostly overlooked in the mainstream literature about transcendental states of mind, was in fact, one of the major paths, if not *the* major pathway, to levels of higher consciousness. Moreover, two of the better known and most powerful instances of illumination recorded in the last 100 years, those of Gopi Krishna and Jiddu Krishnamurti, were directly attributable to kundalini. With such considerations in mind, I was irresistibly drawn to inquire deeper into this adventure called kundalini. This text is the outgrowth of that inquiry.

My purposes in this book are to conceptualize kundalini by describing it as portrayed in the ancient religious texts of India and as depicted in other cultures; to examine kundalini as it occurs spontaneously in people today, thereby showing that kundalini truly exists; to focus on both transcendental and pathological manifestations of kundalini; and to show the importance of creating a social environment where this healing phenomenon can flourish in people's lives. In chapter 10 of this text, I turn to two interviews with Gopi Krishna himself, who during his lifetime may have exemplified the transforming power of kundalini more than any other person in this century.

Chapter 2

༄

Classical
Kundalini — Tantra

The classical descriptions of kundalini are found in the ancient Hindu texts called *Tantras*. From these texts the system called *Tantric Yoga* is derived. The Tantras detail the science of kundalini thoroughly and provide one of the best sources for launching an investigation into this phenomenon. Before beginning the study of this esoteric subject, though, it is helpful to first form an idea of what kundalini is. Here is a brief description based upon the Tantric conception.

There are nine psychic centers, called *chakras*, strung along the spine from the base, up the back, to the crown of the head. (Their location is shown in figure 1 on page 6.) Certain nerves leading from other parts of the body are joined in these centers, so that each center, or chakra, functions as a locus for various emotional, mental, and psychic energies. Until kundalini activates them, however, the chakras are more or less dormant. Kundalini itself, is a bioelectric energy that resides in a latent state in the lowest chakra at the base of the spine. When the kundalini energy is activated, as it may be through meditation, for example, it begins to rise up the spine and "turn on" the chakras, thereby opening up various talents, psychic abilities,

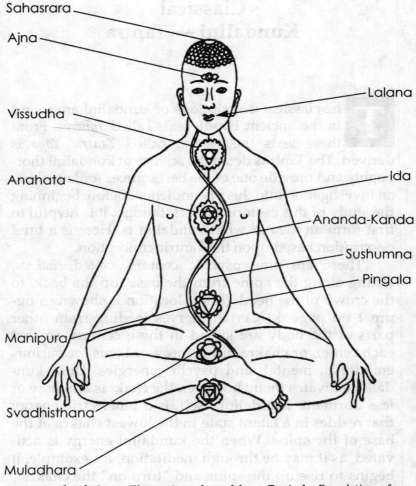

Figure 1. The chakras. (Illustration adapted from Govinda: *Foundations of Tibetan Mysticism.*)

and so forth. Enlightenment occurs when the kundalini energy rises all the way to the top chakra in the crown of the head. One way to visualize this process is to imagine the chakra at the base of the spine as an electric generator and the other chakras as light bulbs varying in wattage from 40 watts at the bottom to 1000 watts at the top. Through certain kinds of meditation or other means described in this book, a switch is thrown, and electricity flows from the generator to one or more of the bulbs, or chakras, lighting them. During enlightenment, electricity streaks all the way to the top bulb. Voilà! The most splendid of all lights flickers on. It is brilliant, multicolored, dazzling—a full 1000 watts. At that "crowning" moment, illumination, enlightenment—union with one's inner self, or the Divine—is achieved.

The Tantras are part of a body of sacred writings called *Shastras*. The Shastras make up the various texts of Hinduism, which include the *Upanishads* and *Puranas*. All are derived from the ancient scriptures, which are called the *Vedas*. The Shastras themselves date back more than 2000 years, and it is from these writings that the different schools of religious philosophy, such as Vedanta, are promulgated. Of these, the system of *Yoga*, dating from the second century B.C., is probably the most familiar to Western culture. The word *Yoga* means union, and refers to union between one's self and the spiritual entity who is not only one's deepest self, but is at the same time the omniscient deity of the universe. Some of the major types of Yoga are:

1) Hatha—Yoga of physical discipline;

2) Bhakti—Yoga of devotion and worship;

3) Karma—Yoga of service and sacrifice;

4) Jnana—Yoga of intellectual understanding;

5) Raja—Yoga of meditation;

6) Tantra—Yoga of Kundalini, which actually is a Jnana Yoga.

Since Kundalini is dealt with so thoroughly in the Tantras this Yoga is sometimes also referred to as Kundalini Yoga. The goal of Kundalini Yoga is ego-transcendence, leading to union with the divine and the concomitant state of blissful consciousness which is called *samadhi*; that is, illumination. This is the same goal that other Yogas set—the methodology, the science of Kundalini Yoga, however, differs dramatically from the others.

The way to understand the roots of this methodology—the deeper dynamics of kundalini ritual and practices, and therefore, the reasoning behind it, is to examine the Tantric cosmology. Tantra is a sophisticated religious philosophy. Behind its symbolic representations of the creator, the act of creation, the universe, and the human personality, lies a penetrating comprehension and a systematic schema of the nature of cosmic forces and of the psyche. This schema, this theory, is not the result of abstract thinking and deduction, but rather is based upon realities directly perceived by the ancient sages. Whether those realities were correctly perceived, is, of course, always open to question. My own purpose is not necessarily to validate Tantric Yoga, but rather to highlight the important features of this cosmology as they refer to kundalini. What follows is a brief summary of the theory of Tantric Yoga.

The Tantric heavens are filled with the Hindu Devas (Gods) and Devis (Goddesses), all of whom are aspects of Brahman, who is the one God, the absolute, the ultimate reality, or pure consciousness. But the Devas and Devis are more than aspects of Brahman, for at the same time, in fact, they *are* the one Brahman—all is Brahman, Brahman is all. Of these deities, two are of primary interest here: Shiva, the masculine and passive element of pure consciousness, and Shakti, the feminine and active element. Shiva and Shakti together form a duality in which Shiva is the power holder, and Shakti is the power itself—Shiva is the great Lord of the universe, and Shakti is the great Mother of the universe. This divine partnership is called the Shiva-Shakti Tattva (attribute). As such, Shiva is the changeless, static aspect of consciousness; Shakti is the ephemeral, kinetic aspect. They are two sides of a coin; therefore, Shiva is in himself Shakti, and Shakti is in herself Shiva. These two are the masculine and feminine forms of Brahman, but in their essence they are still the one Brahman.

Shiva and Shakti are internalized in the human body, although they live separately there. Shakti, the Life Force, resides at the base of the spine. She manifests there as the Devi Kundalini, named after the Sanskrit word *kundala*, meaning coiled, for she has taken the form of a serpent and remains asleep, coiled in the lowest of the seven to nine energy centers of the body, the Muladhara chakra. Since she is a manifestation of Shakti, the Devi Kundalini is also known as Kundalini-Shakti, which is equivalent to saying she is the divine cosmic energy in human beings. Shiva, also dormant in the body, inhabits the Sahasrara chakra (see the chakras in figure 1, page 6), which is located in the crown of the head, and which exists at the furthermost pole from Shakti's abode in the Muladhara chakra. Herein lies the problem, for union with Brahman cannot be achieved so long as Shiva and Shakti are separated. They need each other in order to be activated, to become the one Brahman again. That which is known as the human condition, which is to say, the unhappiness in which people find themselves, can be attributed to this separation in the Shiva-Shakti Tattva, for as such, the psyche is not whole; as such, static and kinetic, masculine and feminine energies are divided, and contact with Brahman, or God, cannot be established. It is the function of the Devi Kundalini to first awaken and then as Shakti to reunite with Shiva, that is, to reconnect the Shiva-Shakti Tattva, so that once again Shiva is Shakti, Shakti is Shiva, the divine pair, joined together in their essence as the one Brahman. This reunion, this completed Yoga (union), therefore, brings the person in whom it occurs into contact with Brahman, which is to say, into a state of enlightenment, samadhi, satori (Zen Buddhist term for illumination), cosmic consciousness, whatever one wants to call it, for he or she who experiences the union of Shakti and Shiva also becomes one with Brahman.

The kundalini process occurs in what is sometimes called the *etheric*, or subtle (nonphysical) body, although as will be demonstrated in chapter 4, this etheric body may actually be physical, composed of atoms and cells just like all other parts of the body. This subtle body is comprised of nerve fibers not visible to the naked eye. For the sake of visualizing this system, therefore, imagine these fibers as looking like all the nerves and ganglia of the nervous system, some as thin and spindly, others as thick and clustery, all of them radiating light, and branching out through the entire body, thousands of them. Their overall appearance in the body might be likened to the grid of electric lights one sees above a city at night. These nerve fibers are actually conduits. They are called *Nadis*; some are major, some are minor, and their function is to conduct currents of energy called *prana*, or vital force, throughout the body. Not only does this prana animate the body, but it is this force that can be controlled by the

Yoga adept through various exercises, described below, to activate the kundalini. Prana, in fact, is kundalini, for kundalini is no more, no less, than prana in a highly potent form. At the present time, of course, science is unaware of the existence of prana or of the Nadi system, although such phenomena have long been known to Tantra and to the world of the occult. Perhaps that is because yogis, mystics, and visionaries have learned how to see with the mind's eye, the mystic third eye of the occult—the eye one uses to view inner imagery. One can hope that in the future, science, too, will develop techniques for viewing and photographing the workings of the Nadis.

At the center of this vast network of Nadi conduits lies the *kundalini plexus*, running from the spine to the head. This is a network comprising the channels through which the kundalini energy flows. It can be compared to the caduceus carried by the winged Hermes, messenger of the Gods in Greek mythology (Mercury in Roman Mythology) and adopted by the medical profession as its insignia. (See figure 2.) The caduceus, in fact, is the ideal symbol with which to accurately visualize the kundalini plexus. At the center of the emblem is a staff representing the *Sushumna* channel, which is a major energy Nadi running from the coccyx to the cerebrum. Around the staff, or Sushumna channel, are intertwined two serpents, symbolizing two other major Nadis: 1) *Ida*, sometimes

Figure 2. The caduceus.

called the *lunar* channel, which begins its upward spiral from the bottom left side of the spine to the right nostril; and 2) *Pingala,* also called the *solar* channel, which begins its upward journey from the bottom right side of the spine to the left nostril. (Note that this network also may be seen in figure 1 on page 6.) Ida is a conductor of negative pranic currents, and Pingala conducts positive pranic currents. The wings at the top of the caduceus may be assigned various meanings. They may represent the flight of Kundalini-Shakti to Shiva and ultimately to Brahman, or they may represent the mystic third eye, since they are reminiscent of the 6th psychic center, the Ajna chakra, which is situated between the eyebrows at the site of the third eye. At the apex of the staff sits a small ball, similar to the ball at the top of a barber pole. This may designate the Sahasrara chakra, already noted, where the Shiva-Shakti Tattva is reinstated to become once again the one Brahman.

Not shown on the caduceus are the chakras, briefly described at the beginning of this chapter, shown in figure 1, and discussed in detail in chapter 4. The chakras form an integral part of the kundalini plexus and figure significantly in Tantric cosmology. They are centers located at various junctures along the Sushumna through which Kundalini-Shakti must eventually pass on her long journey to reunite with Shiva. Of course, the Devi may first doze for centuries, i.e., for many lifetimes. But the day does come, when for one reason or another, she is finally aroused from her dormancy. She then proceeds to rise up the Sushumna and awaken, or open, the chakras. Each chakra represents an obstacle that must be surmounted; each one is a vortice of psychic energy that must be activated—a passageway waiting to be lit by the light of understanding. As the chakras are penetrated by the kundalini energy, transfiguration occurs, for each chakra is governed by its own dynamic, where various emotions, both pleasurable and unpleasurable, are encountered, where illusions are stripped of their facades, where emotional knots are untied, and where understanding is increased. But the journey is over only when the top chakra, the Sahasrara, is awakened, for only there can the Devi Kundalini and the Deva Shiva be united. So the kundalini uncoils and enters the innermost channel of the Sushumna. Inside the Sushumna, there are three other channels: the Vajra, inside of which is the Chitrini, inside of which is the Brahmanadi. It is into this Brahmanadi that the kundalini energy moves as it begins its ascent. The kundalini rises, and then, in a culminating moment of ecstasy, the Devi reaches the Sahasrara chakra—Shakti is reunited with Shiva, and the individual consciousness is transformed.

Thus, as the preceding synopsis illustrates, the main focus of Tantric Yoga is on the arousal of kundalini. And this emphasis is by no means theoretical, nor does it apply to the mere study of a system of abstract ideas. For underlying the entire philosophy is the conviction that the kundalini energy can be awakened by the systematic practice of various exercises. To this end meditational techniques have been developed that involve breathing (Pranayama), Yogic postures (Asanas), hand positions and gestures (Mudras), syllabic chanting (Mantras), muscular contractions (Bandhas), sexual rites (Tantra-Asana), although infrequent, and the use of herbs (Aushadhi), also infrequent. Practical application of any or all of these techniques is the primary *raison d'être* of Tantric Yoga.

In the West, perhaps in the East also, Tantric Yoga has drawn to itself the appellation, the sexual Yoga. The sexual rites do exist, it is true, although they are aimed at the awakening of kundalini, not orgasm. Even so, such rites are rarely practiced, and in any case are reserved only for especially selected, advanced initiates. Kundalini scholar Gene Kieffer argues that Tantra-Asana was developed centuries ago as a subterfuge, as a means to obscure the real techniques of kundalini arousal from initiates who had less than honorable, spiritual motives and who sought only the power that kundalini can bestow upon an individual. There does exist a close concourse between sexual energy and the kundalini energy, which will be explored later in this text, but the similarity is not related to the sexual act itself. Kieffer points out, reasonably enough, that sexual excitation can only culminate in its intended goal— orgasm, not enlightenment. The technique of Aushadhi, which uses hallucinogefcnic herbs, on the other hand, can awaken kundalini, although here too, the practice is taught only to a select few. It should be emphasized, also, that such usage is restricted to herbs, not drugs. Nevertheless, the corollaries that can be inferred between sexual arousal and kundalini arousal, the eso-teric cosmology of the Tantric metaphysic, and the shroud of mystery that envelops the word *kundalini* itself, all have combined to cast this Yoga in a question-able light.

It remains to be seen whether Tantra will ever rid itself of the skepticism with which it has come to be regarded. Humanity might be better off if it does, for Tantra may harbor some of the solutions the world so desperately needs. When seen without preconceptions, Tantric Yoga and the kundalini that is its heartbeat appear as worthy alternatives to the stagnant rituals of worship that characterize many religions. For in the embrace that is finally exchanged between Kundalini-Shakti and Shiva, a dynamic emerges that has the power to eliminate human anguish and to restore a sense of joy to the human spirit. That dynamic is kundalini.

Chapter 3

Contemporary Kundalini

At the close of chapter 1, I spoke of kundalini as an adventure. It is in fact an internal adventure, and the following pages dramatically portray the kinds of encounters that may greet the inward voyager. The four stories told here are original and tell of a moment in time when each of the dramatis personae came to know viscerally the extraordinary phenomenon called kundalini. These are tales of wonder and many will undoubtedly find them inspiring and helpful in shaping their own spiritual direction, in bolstering their own faith that there is a universal purpose underlying the human experience. Others, including those who have unexpectedly found themselves traveling inwardly in dimensions for which they were unprepared, and those who ordinarily would not apply themselves to esoteric or occult subjects, may find spiritual realities depicted in these pages worthy of serious thought and reflection. For these chronicles are not just a depiction of the energy called kundalini, they are also journals about survival in the remote, deeper realms of one's being.

GOPI KRISHNA

Gopi Krishna was living in the city of Jammu, the winter capital of the states of Jammu and Kashmir in northern

India, when kundalini first became active in his body. The year was 1937. He was employed as a clerk under the Director of Education in the Public Works Department of the state. Gopi Krishna was 34 years old. Outside the workplace, it was his custom to spend his time learning about the scriptures and literature of various religions and in the study and practice of Yoga. His practice included rising early every morning so that he could meditate in the early light of dawn. While meditating, he would contemplate "an imaginary lotus in full bloom, radiating light," and would sit "steadily, unmoving and erect, [his] thoughts uninterruptedly centered on the lotus."[1] One December morning, his meditation took an unexpected turn. As he described it:

My whole being was so engrossed in the con-templation of the lotus that for several minutes at a time I lost touch with my body and sur-roundings. During such intervals I used to feel as if I were poised in mid-air, without any feel-ing of a body around me. The only object of which I was aware was a lotus of brilliant colour, emitting rays of light....

During one such spell of intense concentra-tion, I suddenly felt a strange sensation below the base of the spine, at the place touching the seat, while I sat cross-legged on a folded blan-ket spread on the floor. The sensation was so extraordinary and so pleasing that my attention was forcibly drawn towards it. The moment my attention was thus unexpectedly withdrawn from the point on which it was focused, the sen-sation ceased. Thinking it to be a trick played by my imagination to relax the tension, I dis-missed the matter from my mind and brought my attention back to the point from which it had wandered. Again I fixed it on the lotus, and as the image grew clear and distinct at the top of my head, again the sensation occurred. This time I tried to maintain the fixity of my attention and succeeded for a few seconds, but the sensation extending upwards grew so intense and was so extraordinary, as compared to anything I had experienced before, that in spite of myself my mind went towards it, and at that very moment it again disappeared. . . . My heart began to beat wildly, and I found it difficult to bring my attention to the required degree of fixity. After a while I grew composed and was soon as deep in meditation as before. When completely immersed I again experienced the sensation, but this time, instead of allowing my mind to leave the point where I had fixed it, I maintained a rigidity of attention throughout. The sensation again extended upwards, growing in intensity, and I felt myself wavering; but with a great effort I kept my attention centered round the lotus. Suddenly, with a roar like that of a waterfall, I felt a stream of liquid light entering my brain through the spinal cord.

Entirely unprepared for such a development, I was completely taken by surprise; but regaining self-control instantaneously, I remained sitting in the same posture, keeping my mind on the point of concentration. The illumination grew brighter and brighter, the roaring louder, I experienced a rocking sensation and then felt myself slipping out of my body, entirely enveloped in a halo of light. It is impossible to describe the experience accurately. I felt the point of my consciousness that was myself growing wider, surrounded by waves of light. It grew wider and wider, spreading outward while the body, normally the immediate object of its perception, appeared to have receded into the distance until I became entirely unconscious of it. I was now all consciousness, without any outline, without any idea of a corporeal appendage, without any feeling or sensation coming from the senses, immersed in a sea of light simultaneously conscious and aware of every point, spread out, as it were, in all directions without any barrier or material obstruction. I was no longer myself, or to be more accurate, no longer as I knew myself to be, a small point of awareness confined in a body, but instead was a vast circle of consciousness in which the body was but a point, bathed in light and in a state of exaltation and happiness impossible to describe.

After some time, the duration of which I could not judge, the circle began to narrow down; I felt myself contracting, becoming smaller and smaller, until I again became dimly conscious of the outline of my body, then more clearly; and as I slipped back to my old condition, I became suddenly aware of the noises in the street, felt again my arms and legs and head, and once more became my narrow self in touch with body and surroundings. When I opened my eyes and looked about, I felt a little dazed and bewildered, as if coming back from a strange land completely foreign to me.[2]

At first Gopi Krishna doubted his own senses about what had occurred. He wondered if he had been hallucinating.

He dared not think it possible that he could have been given a glimpse of the "transcendental," a vision of divinity, that he, Gopi Krishna, had apprehended "reality." Yet, to the contrary, it seemed that he had, in fact, just undergone a full-blown kundalini experience. He recalled having read about kundalini in books on Yoga. Generally, he knew what kundalini was; he had heard about this strange force sometimes called the serpent power, or the serpent fire. Still, it was hard to believe that he could have been one of the select few lucky enough to stumble upon the key to the esoteric mechanism called kundalini. Self-doubt notwithstanding, there had been unquestionably an expansion of self, of his own consciousness, that seemed to have been brought about by a powerful current starting from below his spine and running to his brain through his backbone. He was compelled to admit that the light he had experienced was not that of the sun that he afterwards had found risen and playing upon his face—instead, this light was internal, an integral part of enlarged consciousness, a part of his very own self. Gopi Krishna could not deny, in spite of his own skepticism, that he had just passed through a superconsciousness state of mind.

Contrary to the idealized version of enlightenment, Gopi Krishna did not remain in a state of nirvana after activating the kundalini—he did not become an overnight sage dispensing wisdom from the heights of the Himalayas. Quite the opposite. For, as he himself described it, he had released a stormy force in his body. The day following his initial experience, he was again able to arouse the kundalini, with similar results, although this time the feeling of exaltation was not as strong and did not last as long. Afterward he felt depressed, even despondent; in fact, a cloud of depression and gloom, a condition of horror was gradually starting to settle upon him for he was starting to see strange internal sights and apparitions. This was a world he had not known existed, it was frightening—abnormal. He began to suspect that he stood not at the gates of enlightenment, but rather that he had arrived at the border of a vast chasm called madness. Worse than that, Gopi Krishna began to realize that perhaps he had taken one irrevocable step too many, for already he was dangling over the edge, "suspended by a thread, swinging between life on the one hand and death on the other, between sanity and insanity, between light and darkness, between heaven and earth."[3]

Gopi Krishna spent the third day after his "awakening" in bed. He was unable to focus his thoughts for any length of time and a thin stream of a radiant essence was steadily pouring into his brain with a sinister light. The days that followed were nightmarish, and he lost the urge to meditate. He was unable to eat normally and finally was reduced to a cup or two of milk and a few oranges each day. His reading was desultory, for he could not maintain concentration. The nights were impossible. No sooner would he close his eyes than a large tongue of flame would leap across his spine into his head. The intensity of the stream of light running from his spinal cord into his brain grew greater during the night. Whenever he closed his eyes he was confronted by a weird circle of light and swirling luminous currents. The spectacle had an aura of the supernatural that chilled him to the bone. Gazing inward, he found himself in the midst of an overwhelming fireworks display; he was surrounded by roaring sounds, showers of light, and waves of copper color stretching out into the darkness all around him. Gopi Krishna's world had become incomprehensible. His feeling for the wife and children he loved so dearly disappeared. At night in his bedroom, satanic creatures with disfigured faces and twisted, inhuman forms leered at him from the darkness. From within he was devoured by fire as if a furnace were raging inside; red-hot pins assailed his body, "scorching and blistering the organs and tissues like flying sparks."[4] In the depths of his being he was filled with dread and fear.

During this period, which lasted more than two months, Gopi Krishna kept the seriousness of what he knew to be a life-and-death struggle from his wife. Neither did he consult a psychiatrist, for he felt that his mental state was beyond the scope and ken of psychotherapy, and he recognized that a single mistake in treatment might prove fatal. He mentioned his condition to his brother-in-law who, though unable to offer any answers himself, did provide the clue that led ultimately to his recovery. The brother-in-law stated that his own guru had remarked that if kundalini is awakened through the Pingala Nadi on the right side of the Sushumna channel, that one can be burned to death through excessive *internal* heat. As might be expected, this bit of information did not appear particularly revelatory at the moment, and in fact, terrified Gopi Krishna even further. As a result he consulted a learned ascetic from Kashmir. The ascetic proved to be a great disappointment, however, suggesting that the malady might be due to malignant spirits. It seemed there were no answers to his dilemma.

Toward the end of February 1938, on the eve of the holy festival of Shivrati (Night of Shiva), this phase of the kundalini process reached its climax. Gopi Krishna had taken to bed. Every part of his body was burning. He felt that he was dying. Then he remembered his brother-in-law's counsel about the Pingala Nadi. Here is Gopi Krishna's description of what happened next:

. . . as if by divine dispensation the idea flashed across my brain to make a last-minute attempt to rouse *Ida,* or the lunar nerve on the left side, to activity, thus neutralizing the dreadful burning effect of the devouring fire within. . . . I brought my attention to bear on the left side of the seat of Kundalini, and tried to force an imaginary cold current upward through the middle of the spinal cord . . . . I distinctly felt the location of the nerve and strained hard mentally to divert its flow into the central channel. Then, as if waiting for the destined moment, a miracle happened.

There was a sound like a nerve thread snapping and instantaneously a silvery streak passed zigzag through the spinal cord, exactly like the sinuous movement of a white serpent in rapid flight, pouring an effulgent, cascading shower of brilliant vital energy into my brain, filling my head with a blissful lustre in place of the flame. . . . Completely taken by surprise at this sudden transformation and . . . overjoyed at the cessation of pain, I remained absolutely quiet and motionless for some time, tasting the bliss of relief with a mind flooded with emotion, unable to believe I was really free of the horror . . . . I immediately fell asleep, bathed in light and for the first time after weeks of anguish felt the sweet embrace of restful sleep.[5]

Gopi Krishna awoke after about an hour. The blissful lustre was still streaming through his head; his heart and pulse were normal, and the burning sensations and fear had all but vanished. Truly hungry for the first time in weeks, he asked his wife for a cup of milk and some bread, then fell asleep again. After two hours he awoke in the same exalted state of mind. He observed the appearance of the lustrous radiance in his stomach, a golden flame searching for food. Then he took some more bread and milk. To his surprise he found that the lustre in his head contracted simultaneously as the golden flame in the stomach expanded—as if some of the energy streaming through his brain were being drawn off to the gastric region to assist in digestion. Eventually the radiance moved throughout the digestive tract, "caressing the intestines and the liver, while another stream poured into the kidneys and the heart."[6] The current flowed through his body autonomously; he was powerless to direct it in any way and merely watched passively, incredibly, deeply happy. It seemed that he had made a transition to a new phase in the kundalini process. Gopi Krishna wrote:

> I felt no discomfort now; all that I could feel was
> a gentle and soothing warmth moving through
> my body as the current travelled from point to
> point. I watched this wonderful play silently,
> my whole being filled with boundless gratitude
> to the Unseen for this timely deliverance from a
> dreadful fate; and a new assurance began to
> shape itself in my mind that the serpent fire was
> in reality now at work in my exhausted and
> agonized body; and that I was safe.[7]

It took twelve years for the kundalini to become integrated into Gopi Krishna's bodily and mental processes. After the initial crisis had passed, he remained generally in good health, but there were still many crises to go through. It was necessary to adhere to a rigorous diet and regular habits of sleep; and those times when he did abandon his daily or nightly regimen, he paid for it severely, once suffering a relapse so serious, it brought him all the way back to where he had started—trembling with fear, near death, burning within, encircled by an internal wall of fire. Gopi Krishna was learning to cope though, and he always recovered from such temporary reversals with the luminous glow in his brain intact.

Gradually, Gopi Krishna began to observe a metamorphosis in the world around him. Buildings now appeared to be lit with a brilliant silvery lustre, scenes before his eyes were magnified in a rich blend of color and shade, and objects shone with a milky lustre indicative of a new phase of kundalini. Gopi Krishna summed it up: ". . . an extraordinary change had taken place in the now luminous cognitive centre in my brain . . . the fascinating lustre which I perceived around every object, was not a figment of my fancy nor was it possessed by the objects, but [was] a projection of my own internal radiance."[8]

Years passed, and the dramatic metamorphosis in the outside world remained. Gopi Krishna's health was fully restored. His mind functioned well, he could read for long periods without fatigue, and he returned to a normal diet. The only reminder of his ordeals was that he continued to take a cup of milk every morning and again in the afternoon with a slice of bread. He played chess. "In spite of all these signs of normality," Gopi Krishna wrote, "it was easy to perceive that mentally I was not the same old self. The lustre within and without became more and more perceptible with the passage of time. With my inner vision I could distinctly perceive the flow of lucent currents of vital energy through the network of nerves in my body. A living silvery flame with a delicate golden tinge was clearly perceptible in the interior of my brain across the forehead. My thought images were vividly bright, and every object recalled to memory possessed radiance in the same manner as in the concrete form."[9]

JIDDU KRISHNAMURTI

When he was only 4 years old, Jiddu Krishnamurti was spotted on a beach in Adyar, a suburb of Madras, India, by Charles Webster Leadbeater. Leadbeater was one of the early leaders of the Theosophical Society, an international religious organization headquartered in Madras. After observing the young boy on several occasions, Leadbeater, who was reputed to have clairvoyant powers, reported that Krishnamurti had a remarkable aura and that one day he would be a great spiritual teacher. Leadbeater brought the young boy to the attention of the theosophical hierarchy, presided over by Annie Besant, well known in her day as a writer, lecturer, social thinker, and advocate of women's rights. Leadbeater and Besant became convinced that Krishnamurti was destined to be the future leader of Theosophy and on a larger scale that he was to become the "World Teacher." It was 1899, and British colonial power was strong in India. The theosophists, who were decidedly British—the leadership of the organization was British and Besant and Leadbeater were both British—were not above using this power. They conspired to wrest the young boy and his brother Nitya away from the custody of their family, and were successful in this, settling the case in the British courts. Thereafter, the two boys were raised abroad, where they were treated like royalty. They were educated in London and Paris, and Annie Besant became like a mother to them. Incredibly, Krishnamurti did grow up to become a world spiritual teacher, but his teachings were a far cry from what Leadbeater and Besant had envisioned. His teachings, in fact, were the very antithesis of theosophy.

By the time Krishnamurti grew to manhood, the Theosophical Society had become a vast organization with a worldwide membership numbering in the tens of thousands. There were hundreds of Theosophical Lodges, or Centers, various trusts, funds, and estates, an official monthly publication called *The Theosophist*, and a number of internal organizations such as The Order of the Star in the East. This latter organization was created primarily for the dissemination of propaganda about the coming World Teacher, Krishnamurti, and had its own quarterly magazine, *The Herald of the Star*. The Order of the Star was founded by Leadbeater and Besant and was considered an important part of the preparations being made for Krishnamurti's eventual ascension to the leadership of the entire society. On October 17, 1922, however, an event transpired that led ultimately to Krishnamurti's rejection of Theosophy and of the scepter and throne that were to have been his just for the spiritual asking.

It began on Thursday, August 17, 1922, with an odd harbinger of spiritual awakening—a painful lump about the size of a large marble in the middle of the nape of Krishnamurti's neck. He had been staying in a cottage nestled in the midst of apricot orchards and orange groves in the Ojai valley in southern California. Also living in the cottage was his brother Nitya. Mr. A. P. Warrington, the General Secretary of the Theosophical Society in America was quartered in another cottage several hundred yards away. Other than an occasional guest in a Bishop Walton, Vicar-General of the Liberal Catholic Church for America, the three had their end of the valley to themselves.

Krishnamurti had been meditating for about thirty minutes every morning, and for a period of three weeks had been concentrating to hold in his mind the image of the Lord Maitreya[10] throughout the entire day. This he had been able to do without difficulty.

The morning after the lump appeared on Krishnamurti's neck, he became very ill, and was found tossing and groaning in bed by Rosalind Williams, a 19-year-old woman friend of Nitya's, who had been a frequent visitor at the cottage. Krishnamurti was undergoing fits of shivering and trembling, and complained of intense heat. He was in great pain, seemed only half-conscious, and began to have out-of-body experiences. For three days he remained in this condition, attended by Nitya, Rosalind, and Mr. Harrington. Rosalind was especially helpful, holding and comforting Krishnamurti, and it fell to her to nurse him through this ordeal.

Although Krishnamurti was in great distress, there were moments of relief—even rapture. This was illustrated by the first of his out-of-body experiences, during which he saw a man working on the road—but the workman was Krishnamurti himself; the pickaxe the workman held was Krishnamurti himself; the very road which he was repairing was a part of Krishnamurti; the grass itself and the tree beside the workman were Krishnamurti's very self. It was almost as if he had the same thoughts and feelings as the workman. The wind blowing through the trees, the birds, the dust on the road, an ant crawling on a blade of grass—all were Krishnamurti. A car was driving along the road and Krishnamurti became the car; he was the driver, the motor, and the wheels; as the car drove away from Krishnamurti, he found that he was going away from himself. He was part of everything, the orchard groves, the fields, the mountains, the animals, and all living things. He remained in this condition for the entire day, until about six o'clock, when he began to lose awareness of his physical body. At that point, the entity that Krishnamurti called "the elemental"[11] took over and did what it liked; he became semiconscious.[12]

By Sunday the heat had increased and the trembling had grown worse. He didn't want to touch anyone, nor did he want to be touched by anyone. He was exhausted and weeping. His head felt as though many needles had been hammered in. He perceived the bed on which he had been lying as filthy, and he would not lie on it. He complained of dirt, dirt everywhere, the dirt of everyone around him.[13] That evening, Krishnamurti, Nitya, Mr. Warrington, Bishop Walton, and Rosalind had all gathered on the verandah. Krishnamurti sat away from them muttering incoherently. The group was tense, but expectant, as if a momentous event were about to occur. Eventually, at Mr. Harrington's request, Krishnamurti went out under a pepper tree in front of the house. It was dark by then. The tree was lush, the scent of its blossoms filled the air; overhead the leaves were outlined against the starry sky. Krishnamurti then began to meditate. After a while, he found himself going out of his body again. He could see himself sitting down with the leaves of the pepper tree overhead. He was facing East. In the heavens, the Star of the East was brightly shining. Then he felt the Lord Buddha's vibration; he saw the Lord Maitreya and Master K. H.[14] Krishnamurti felt indescribably happy and peaceful. He hovered near his body and within himself he had a sense of a calm, placid lake of infinite depth.[15] Nothing would ever be the same again for Krishnamurti; he had transcended pain and sorrow—he had seen the light. Later, he would write, "I have drunk at the fountain of joy and eternal Beauty. I am God-intoxicated."[16]

Krishnamurti began to chant. This was followed by a period of silence and the group finally heard Krishnamurti coming up to the house out of the darkness. The crisis had passed.

The symptoms recurred August 21st, although they now lasted only a few minutes at a time. Nitya wrote that Krishnamurti lay in samadhi all day, under the pepper tree, and at night he sat in meditation as he had the previous evening. Both Nitya and Rosalind placed an extremely mystical interpretation on these events, reporting unseen masters and cosmic music.

Shortly after these incidents, Krishnamurti wrote Annie Besant, whom he addressed as Mother, that he had gotten back into the consciousness of the Masters, that he had regained his old touch with the Lord Maitreya, and that now he hoped to help the world climb a few feet higher. He informed her that he was now slightly clairvoyant as the result of all that had transpired.

In a second letter, written on September 16th to Lady Emily Lutyens, International Lecturer for the Theosophical Society and a trusted friend and confidante, he was more candid, revealing how tumultuous those days had been and continued to be for him. He wrote:

> . . . I toss about, groan & moan and mutter strange things, in fact almost behave like one possessed. I get up, thinking somebody is calling me and collapse on the floor; I rave considerably, see strange faces & light. . . . All the time, I have a violent pain in my head & the nape of my neck. Also during that time, I become very sensitive, can't bear a sound, however small it may be. . . . now it has lasted for nearly a month, practically everyday. . . . I may become clairvoyant when it is all over or merely that I am gradually going mad!!![17]

The events in Ojai marked a turning point in Krishnamurti's spiritual life. At first, Krishnamurti and those around him tried to interpret these events within the context of theosophical beliefs and expectations. But eventually, the incidents that made these days so remarkable were simply called "the process." This process continued on a daily basis until September 25th, when it stopped temporarily. Nitya wrote that around 6:30 every evening Krishnamurti would fall into a semi-comatose state for about an hour-and-a-half. During this time, the personality known as Krishnamurti would recede into the background and the elemental would take over the bodily functions, including communicating bits of mundane information pertaining to the care of the body. Since Krishnamurti complained of acute pain in the spine when he was in this condition, Nitya and the others in the inner group concluded that the process signified the awakening of kundalini.[18]

In discussing Krishnamurti's condition, Leadbeater wrote to Annie Besant on May 12, 1923: "I do not understand why such terrible physical suffering should come to our Krishna. . . . I have no recollection of anything in the least commensurate with this when I was passing through the same stage, though there was certainly a great deal of excessive discomfort in the development of the Kundalini."[19] Krishnamurti did suffer excessively during the process; but as soon as a "session" had ended he would return to his usual self and go about his business without undue concern.

Typically, the process was attended by: excruciating pain in the spine, head, and neck; out-of-body experiences; burning at the nape of the neck and base of the spine; fainting, groaning, shivering, and weeping; and the perception that unseen presences were working on his body, opening it, and preparing it for greater spiritual service—Krishnamurti was to say that "they" had left open the center in his Brahman Gate[20] and eventually he reported that he could leave his body with ease.

The process continued on and off into the following year and beyond. By February 7, 1924, Nitya informed Mrs. Besant that the process had been ongoing for seventy-six days straight, and that though Krishnamurti's pain had intensified over time, he had developed a greater capacity to bear it. Finally, on February 27th, the process reached its culmination. Except for the reference to the vision of "The Lord," Krishnamurti biographer Pupul Jayakar called the following account by Krishnamurti "a classic description of the arousing of the *kundalini*."[21] Here is Krishnamurti's statement:

> Whatever it is, the force or whatever one calls the bally thing, came up my spine, up to the nape of my neck, then it separated into two, one going to the right & the other to the left of my head till they met between the two eyes, just above my nose. There was a kind of flame & I saw the Lord & the Master. It was a tremendous night. Of course the whole thing was painful, in the extreme. Last night, I was too tired to have anything done but I suppose it will continue. . . .[22]

Krishnamurti's characterization of the kundalini current as "the bally thing" seems brash, almost irreverent, yet it is consistent with his general attitude during these trying times. For in spite of extreme pain, he was essentially cheerful and remained undaunted in spirit throughout the unfolding of the process. This was fortunate, because the process continued to shadow Krishnamurti for the rest of his life.

For the next five-and-a-half years Krishnamurti struggled with the process and the conflict between his own emerging message and the ideals and beliefs of theosophy. Then on August 3, 1929, he officially dissolved the Order of the Star, of which he had become president, and left the Theosophical Society forever. At the same time, he eschewed the masters and rejected religious dogma and beliefs entirely. "I maintain that Truth is a pathless land," he proclaimed, "and you cannot approach it by any path whatsoever, by any religion, by any sect. That is my point of view, and I adhere to that absolutely and unconditionally."[23]

The process continued year after year. Whatever calendar page one turns in the diary of Krishnamurti's life, one finds the process. Here is an entry reported by Pupul Jayakar in 1948:

> ... Krishnamurti started saying that he was very hurt inside that they had burnt him inside; that there was a pain right through his head. ...
> He kept on feeling his body to see if it was all there. He said: "I must go back and find out what had happened on the walk. Something happened and they rushed back. But, I do not know whether I returned? There may be pieces of me lying in the road."[24]

It seems appropriate to close an account of Krishnamurti's life with this story. For eventually one realizes after piecing together those bits and fragments lying on the road with all the other bizarre facets of his life that they form no more than a gigantic question mark. But perhaps, after all, that is a satisfactory answer to a life that was always enigmatic and always mystical.

In summing up, the record clearly indicates that it was kundalini that lit the way to the measureless toward which Krishnamurti never ceased pointing. Yet, the process that was intrinsic to Krishnamurti's sense of the

absolute, of the timeless, was always painful in its manifestation. But there was another side to the process, for
alongside the pain there were the states of exaltation,
bliss, and that silence of which Krishnamurti spoke—
something immense, too vast to put into words. It is this
immensity, this sense of the absolute, that are the heart
and soul of Krishnamurti's message.

By the end of his life, Krishnamurti had become completely acclimatized to the process. He described it as a
normal everyday thing. It was not, however, something he
sought or invited through meditation or unconscious longing—he had no desire to achieve anything. On the contrary, it was as if the process pursued him, waking him in
the middle of the night with what he called, "that peculiar
meditation." He did not try to summon the experience of
such meditations from his memory, so each meditation
was fresh and new. Sometimes the meditations were
accompanied by intense pain in his head; sometimes he
awoke with a sense of boundless space, and of surging,
immeasurable energy; other times he woke up laughing
and with indescribable joy. Meditations like these occurred
almost nightly as Krishnamurti approached the end of his
life, growing ever more powerful with the passing years.
Only when he was traveling would the meditations
cease.[25] Here is his own third person description, written
when he was 84 years old:

> With the arrival in Rishi Valley in the middle of
> November 1979 the momentum increased and
> one night in the strange stillness of that part of
> the world, with the silence undisturbed by the
> hoot of owls, he woke up to find something
> totally different and new. The movement had
> reached the source of all energy. This must in no
> way be confused with, or even thought of, as

god or the highest principle, the Brahman,
which are the projections of the human mind
out of fear and longing, the unyielding desire
for total security. It is none of those things.
Desire cannot possibly reach it, words cannot
fathom it nor can the string of thought wind
itself around it. One may ask with what assur-
ance do you state that it is the source of all
energy? One can only reply with complete
humility that it is so.[26]

HIROSHI MOTOYAMA

Dr. Hiroshi Motoyama was taught to chant Buddhist
sutras and Shintō prayers by his natural and foster mothers when he was just 4 years old. The two mothers and the
young boy would chant for hours without cessation. Both
of the mothers were advanced spiritual devotees, and they
raised the young child in a religious environment. They
used to take him on spiritual pilgrimages to the temples
and shrines in the mountains of Shōdō Island in Kagawa
Prefecture, Japan, where he was born. From these two
women he reports that he learned about and experienced
the existence of non-human entities who inhabit the higher
dimensions. He was also taken to places reputed to be
high energy centers for the practice of various kinds of religious asceticism. With such a background, it was no surprise when he grew up to become a serious student of
Yoga, nor that he had awakened kundalini by the time he
was 25 years old.

The young Motoyama undertook a rigorous discipline right off. He would arise at 3:00 in the morning to
practice Asanas (Yogic postures) for a half hour, and
then meditate for the next three or four hours. His meditation consisted of Pranayama (breathing exercises)

and concentration upon specific chakras. He was adept at meditation and obtained some positive results soon after beginning his Yoga studies. For instance, his body and mind began to fill with extraordinary amounts of energy, and symptoms of a stomach disorder and an ear discharge disappeared within six months after he had started the Yoga practices. During continued study and meditation, Motoyama began to notice the first signs of an awakening kundalini. Here is his description:

I began to notice some new sensations. I had an itchy feeling at the coccyx, a tingling feeling on the forehead and at the top of the head, and a feverish sensation in the lower abdomen. I could hear a sound something like the buzzing of bees around the coccyx. In ordinary daily life my sense of smell became so sensitive that I could not endure offensive odors.

These conditions continued for two or three months. One day, when I was meditating before the altar as usual, I felt particularly feverish in the lower abdomen and saw there a round blackish-red light like a ball of fire about to explode in the midst of a white vapor. Suddenly, an incredible power rushed through my spine to the top of the head and, though it lasted only a second or two, my body levitated off the floor a few centimeters. I was terrified. My whole body was burning, and a severe headache prevented me from doing anything all day. The feverish state continued for two or three days. I felt as if my head would explode with energy. Hitting myself around the "Brahman Gate" at the top of the head was the only thing that brought relief.

This, then, was the first time I had experienced the rising of the kundalinī shakti to the top of my head through the sushumnā. I did not experience as much physical or mental difficulty as is so often associated with this experience, probably because of the fortunate fact that my Brahman Gate was already open and the shakti was able to flow out into the astral dimension.[27]

Motoyama connects this initial kundalini experience to the awakening of the Muladhara chakra. In fact, he describes all his kundalini experiences in the context of the chakras.

Dr. Motoyama then proceeds to describe the activation of all the chakras. In the text he places the chakras in their usual order, from bottom to top—from the Muladhara to the Sahasrara—but he points out that in actuality, he awakened the Muladhara, Svadhisthana, Manipura, and Sahasrara chakras before the others. (See figure 1 on p. 6 illustrating the location of all the chakras.) Motoyama believes that the sequence of chakra awakening varies from person to person. He ascribes this to differing karma and nature among individuals. This affects the ease or difficulty by which a particular chakra may be opened. In Dr. Motoyama's descriptions, the chakras are the poles to which the kundalini current is drawn. He portrays the chakras as an integral part of the kundalini process and contends that enlightenment cannot be reached until one has awakened and recognized the chakras. Dr. Motoyama says that this contention is also stated in one of the Upanishads. He does not, however, mention the two minor chakras, the Ananda-Kanda and the Lalana, in this context, for he does not consider minor chakras to be centers of awakening.

The Svadhisthana was the next chakra to open after the Muladhara and first appeared to Dr. Motoyama as a round, crimson fireball in his abdomen. This was accompanied by prophetic dreams and telepathic experiences. The awakening of this chakra marked the beginning of a period that Motoyama calls a "dangerous stage"[28] in his practice. During meditation the smallest sound startled him, as if thunder had struck nearby; he would become easily excited and felt that he had become emotionally unstable. He remarks that it is generally advisable to have the guidance of an experienced guru when passing through this juncture. Motoyama himself was fortunate enough to have both his mothers assisting him, each knowledgeable about spiritual matters, and he states that additionally he was shielded by "divine protection,"[29] so he came through this crisis without undue difficulty. He does not mention any instance of kundalini activation in connection with this chakra, although he does report a feverish feeling in the abdomen, like a mixture of ice and fire, accompanied by a vision of white steam; this feeling, however, occurred some months before the initial awakening of kundalini.

About six months after Dr. Motoyama began Yoga meditation he became aware of a new series of sensations. He perceived this as a reddish light centered on the navel; the light would become intensely white, seemingly brighter than the sun. As Dr. Motoyama continued to observe the light he would become dizzy to the extent that he could see nothing for about ten minutes. During these moments, which signaled the opening of the Manipura chakra, he also began to perceive a purple light shining sometimes in his abdomen and other times between his eyebrows.

Dr. Motoyama relates that he had always seen ghosts—what he terms lower astral beings—since his childhood, and during the opening of the Manipura chakra, he began to observe such apparitions with greater frequency when meditating. He states that the ability to interact with the spirit world, communicating with, being influenced by, or influencing various spirits, is demonstrably increased after the Manipura has been activated. Motoyama makes a point of warning that overusing the abilities associated with this chakra, or for that matter, overusing any one chakra to the exclusion of others, can result in disease or abnormalities of both the mind and body. Again, he does not report any kundalini activity in connection with the Manipura chakra.

The opening of the Anahata chakra occurred about two years after Dr. Motoyama had begun Yoga, and here, unlike the Svadisthana and Manipura, he describes the rising of kundalini. He attributes healing ability and fulfillment of personal wishes to the opening of this chakra. His account indicates that the awakening was dramatic.

At this time, as is usual during the coldest period of winter, I was practicing the traditional water asceticism of rising at dawn, going outside, and pouring icy water over my seminaked body for about an hour. As I was doing this, my mother stood by and prayed for me.

One morning the following occurred. I saw a kind of heat energy rising from my coccyx to my heart through the spine. My chest felt very hot and I saw my heart start to shine a brilliant gold. The icy water was warmed by this heat, steam rose from the surface of my body, but I did not feel cold. As the kundalinī rose from my heart to the top of my head, it became shining white. It left my body through the top of my head and I rose with it into a much higher dimension. My physical body was standing in the cold wind of this world, but I had forgotten it. I was half-unconscious, and yet I was aware of being in the heights and of worshiping the Divine. When I came to myself ten to twenty minutes later, my mother told me that she had seen a golden light shining at the top of my head and at my heart. I think this experience is the point at which my anāhata chakra was awakened.[30]

During the fourth and fifth years of Motoyama's practice, he began concentrating on the Vissudha chakra. Shortly thereafter, his throat became irritated and he began to have difficulty in breathing. After a number of months had passed, he became aware one day of a purple light spreading around his head. He lost consciousness of his body. Inside himself all was quiet and calm. He had entered into a state of mind in which there was total still-ness. Motoyama paraphrases a Buddhist saying to com-municate this stillness: ". . . everything, whatever it may be, is subject to change, because all things, once created, have to come to an end. Having transcended birth and death, having gone beyond them, we are in Shūnyatā, the absolute nothingness and the highest good."[31]

Lurking in Shūnyatā, however, were hazards Dr. Motoyama had not anticipated. After entering this state a few times, he found himself at the edge of a precipice, what he calls "an abyss of absolute void."[32] This filled him with such dread that it became an almost insur-mountable impasse. He felt that he might literally die if he had to face that void. He considered giving up Yoga entirely. Paralyzed by fear, he learned to surrender completely to God, as he remembers, "to totally entrust my life to Him."[33] Gradually, he overcame his fear.

But the abyss was not the only peril. Dr. Motoyama describes another danger he faced:

> During this process, I encountered a horrible devil-like being. It was an indescribably terrifying experience. However, I also had the realization that all things, even "gods and devils" are transient; ultimately there is nothing to fear. This realization is what enabled me to pass through this frightening and dangerous period.
>
> When my fear was overcome and 'I could enjoy the feeling of total silence all around me ... I experienced a deeply wonderful feeling of nonattachment and freedom.[34]

Dr. Motoyama states that as a result of an awakened Vissudha his hearing was improved and he could now read the past and future—people's former, present, and future lives appeared to him as one continuous stream. He does not link the Vissudha to kundalini in the text.

The Ajna chakra awakened with comparatively little difficulty, and the passage was smooth and calm. Pranayama was the means by which the kundalini became active.

> After performing [Pranayama] one hour a day for several months, kundalinī energy rose from my coccyx through my spine and my body became hot. My lower abdomen surrounding the svādhisthāna chakra became as hard as iron. My respiration became so easy and slow that I felt as if I could live without breathing. My body, especially the upper half of my torso, felt as though it disappeared. My ājnā chakra began to vibrate very subtly. I was completely

immersed in a dark purple light while a bright white light shone from between my eyebrows. I heard a voice call me as if it were echoing in a valley. I was filled with ecstasy and a divine symbol of power was revealed to me. This state continued for one or two hours and, I think, indicated the initial awakening of the chakra.[35]

Dr. Motoyama had entered what he called a higher dimension of consciousness. He was filled with a "heavenly calm," and writes, "I did not experience the dimming or loss of consciousness that had happened in the awakening of the other chakras. Rather, I found myself in a state of widened and deepened consciousness, a consciousness of a higher dimension sometimes referred to as superconsciousness."[36] Dr. Motoyama found that the past, present, and future were simultaneously knowable, and that he could understand objects in their very essence. There were other insights—the purpose of the karma that people were struggling with, their previous incarnations, and the karma of nations and of the world itself became clear to him. He states that not only could he now see spirits, but that he could be affected by them. He became aware of their suffering and was able to help them by praying to God for their liberation. Dr. Motoyama believes that the power to have an effect upon, to purify the karma of others, is the most important attribute arising from the activation of the Ajna chakra. He asserts that the awakening of both the Ajna and the Sahasrara are absolutely essential to the evolvement of a human being to a higher plane.

When the Sahasrara chakra is awakened the kundalini process has reached its fulfillment. One would expect, therefore, that this chakra would be the last to open. Dr. Motoyama reports, however, that the Sahasrara opened less than a year after he began Yoga. As stated earlier, this was preceded by the Muladhara, Svadhisthana, and the Manipura. The Anahata, Vissudha, and Ajna each became active at a later date.

Dr. Motoyama opened the Sahasrara through a Taoist form of kundalini exercise called Shōshūten, although he does not specify these exercises in the text. Here is his description of the Sahasrara awakening:

> While I was doing Shōshūten, I could see the inside of the sushumnā, the sahasrāra and two or three other chakras shining. After I had practiced yoga for six months or a year, a shining golden light began to enter and leave my body through the top of my head and I felt as if the top of my head protruded ten to twenty centimeters. In the astral, but not the physical dimension, I saw what looked like the head of Buddha, shimmering purple and blue, resting on the top of my own head. There was a golden-white light flowing in and out through the gate on top of the Buddha's crown. Gradually I lost the sensation of my body, but I held a clear awareness of consciousness, of superconsciousness. I could see my spiritual self gradually rise higher and leave my body through the top of my head to be restored in Heaven.
>
> I was able to hear a powerful, but very tender, Voice resounding through the universe. While listening to the Voice, I realized spontaneously my mission, my previous lives, my own spiritual state, and many other things. Then I experienced a truly indescribable state, in which my entire spiritual existence became

totally immersed within an extraordinary calmness. After some time, I felt it imperative that I
return to the physical world. I descended, following the same path, and returned to my body
through the gate at the top of my head. I con-
sciously had to permeate my whole body with
spiritual energy because it was frigid and my
extremities were paralyzed. Finally I was able
to move my hands and feet a little, and normal
sensation gradually returned.[37]

Dr. Motoyama reports that his astral body was able to
depart from his body via the Brahman Gate after he had
awakened the Sahasrara, that he was able to see outside
his own body with his eyes closed during meditation,
and that the abilities gained through awakening the
other chakras had been strengthened too. He noted
other benefits as the Sahasrara became more and more
active in higher dimensions, including being able to
enter into and have an effect upon the bodies of others,
and what he calls "the ability to be granted union with
Divine power."[38]

• • • • • •

The next and final biography is my own. The question
whether my own LSD-induced kundalini experience
should be included in these pages was not easy to
resolve. I felt the need to share my experience, for I felt
that it was rare and was a story that should be told. Still,
I debated whether my particular experience of kundalini
arousal would appear credible when contrasted with the
spiritually attained kundalini awakenings of the luminaries whose stories have just been told. At first I
thought it might seem inappropriate, at the least incon-

gruous, to place the journal of an LSD trip alongside the pilgrimages of men like Gopi Krishna, Jiddu Krishna-murti, and Hiroshi Motoyama, who are among the very illuminati of the spiritual world. Yet, I felt that what I knew of kundalini also had merit. I had arrived at that distant shore with a second-class ticket, true. But I beheld the same sights as the first-class passengers.

The celebrated mythologist Joseph Campbell, who is acknowledged as one of the world's scholars on the history of religious rites and practices, upholds the validity of mystical experience resulting from the use of hallucinogens. He writes:

> In the 1950s R. Gordon Wasson's investigations of the Mexican pre-Columbian mushroom cult (in collaboration with Albert Hofmann, the Swiss chemist renowned for his discovery of LSD in 1943) established beyond question the prominence of hallucinogens in the religious exercises of the whole Mayan-Aztec culture field. The same investigators in conjunction with the classicist, Carl A. P. Ruck, have lately revealed the likelihood of the influence of a hallucinogen (ergot of barley) in the Greek mysteries of Eleusis. Already in 1968, Wasson published his disclosure of the mysterious Vedic sacramental, Soma, as probably a product of the mushroom *Amanita muscaria* (fly agaric). Aldous Huxley's *The Doors of Perception* (1954), describing his own visionary experiences under the influence of mescaline, opened the way to a popular appreciation of the ability of hallucinogens to render perceptions of a quasi, or even truly, mystical profundity. There can be no doubt today that through the use of such sacra-

mentals, revelations indistinguishable from some of those reported of yoga have been experienced. Nor can there be any doubt that the source of the revelations is the psyche of the practitioner—the unconscious, that is to say. They are revelations, that is to say further, of the archetypes of the collective unconscious, elementary ideas *a priori* of the species *Homo sapiens* such as may appear spontaneously no matter where.[39]

Even without the considerable buttressing garnered from Campbell's supportive point of view, I came to the realization that it was valid to print my own story. For the subject under consideration here is kundalini, not how spiritually advanced one is. And I believe that my own experience does carry the hallmark of genuine kundalini arousal. As such it can only be revealing and can only shed additional light upon our subject. If anything, the kundalini activated in my body illustrates that this cosmic force is reserved not just for the sainted few, but on the contrary, is the birthright of every person living on this planet. For at the time that I experienced kundalini I was hardly saintly, nor was I religious. I had, in fact, rejected religious beliefs entirely, including the protestant tenets I had been brought up with, and was an avowed agnostic.

It is important to understand that I experimented with LSD only at the urging of a friend, not as a profligate drug user, that I never again used LSD after the occurrences described below, and that I very definitely do not recommend that anyone attempt to arouse kundalini through the use of drugs.

DARREL IRVING

I knew that by taking a mind-expanding drug I would be entering an unknown country. Had I known, though, how truly vast the uncharted terrain, how extraordinarily powerful the forces I was about to encounter, it is doubtful I would have had the courage to cross that threshold. Within an hour after taking the drug, the magic gateway to the unconscious had already begun to swing imperceptibly open. Then the opaque curtain that ordinarily separates consciousness from the unconscious dissolved and fluttered away in a fine rosy glow, illumining the new world I was entering even as I watched it developing around me. A wave of anxiety swept through me, and I went down on one knee to gather my resources, for I knew there was no turning back now. And then, there on the plush Persian carpet upon which I knelt, I looked up and beheld the majesty and beauty of the room as I had never seen a room before. Everything seemed to glow and vibrate, and there was a wondrous newness to even the most mundane of items, such as a date book or a pen and pencil set lying on a desk. Although the apartment had suddenly become enchanting, I was becoming more deeply apprehensive. I pushed my fear away momentarily, though, held fast to my center, and tried to carry on a normal conversation with my friend who had taken the drug with me.

Very quickly the apartment lost its enchantment and began to seem distorted and ominous. My friend and I had to give up our attempts at conversation and went off by ourselves to deal with the powerful changes going on inside us. A large, uncomfortable lump the size of a fist had formed on the nape of my neck and it was difficult to focus on anything but that lump. The objects in the apartment seemed altered and strange. The colors were deeper, more dramatic; a tapestry on the wall was breathtakingly beautiful, yet at the same time it looked dark and foreboding, and when the weave of the tapestry began to crawl and undulate, it seemed so threatening and monstrous that I fled from it in repugnance. The lamps, the chairs, the tables, the walls glowed eerily; the floors appeared to ripple, the apartment itself seemed to be a living, breathing entity. Finally I retired to one of the bedrooms. An ominous hum filled the room I was in. The hum was primordial and came from no known source; it was just there, omniscient, ominous, intense. I finally gave up all hope of carrying on normally and lay down on the bed. The hum was maddening, but it subsided eventually, as did the lump on the back of my neck, and I began a procession through a series of painful inner storms, each an episode unto itself, each presided over by a furious display of thunder and lightning. Throughout the storms there flowed an interminable display of internal imagery—numbers, abstract forms, cartoon-life figures. Although I can remember few of these images now, I do vaguely recollect a hologram-like flower, perhaps a lily, boldly delineated against a deep black velvety backdrop. For a while everything seemed dirty and squalid, the bedding on which I lay seemed indescribably filthy, the clothes I wore seemed equally vile, and I could not bear to think of touching nor of being touched by anyone. At one point I became aware of a desert island upon which the bedraggled apparition of a man lay dying; I drew no closer, but shuddered and moved on. Most of the images were not so concrete and did not remain stationary long enough for a full apprehension of them. Rather, they were in constant flux and rather overwhelming. Once, during a lull between storms, just when I thought I had found a moment's respite, a fire began to kindle inside me. Quickly the fire fanned into a raging inferno and I suddenly found myself burning from within, surrounded by internal flames. There was no escape, and the fire did not subside until the flames had burned me to the very marrow—the pain was enormous.

My friend was having a hard time too, but was better off and was able to join me occasionally and tune the radio to WPAT in Paterson, the easy-listening station. This was the only station I could listen to as everything else—news, human voices, classical music even—was strident and painful to listen to. But I could drift awhile on the easy-listening music, the velvet-string sounds of WPAT. Internally though, further storms were brewing on the horizon, and the deafening thunderclaps and lightning that flashed across the internal sky shook me to the depths of my being, for I was the lightning and I was the thunder. Hours were passing, and I reminded myself constantly that in a few more hours when the drug had worn off I would be out of this. I prayed for that moment to come.

If I were to describe my state of mind at that time, it would be to say that it felt as if I had lost control of my own mental processes, for I had not the slightest idea where the interminable stream of images flowing through my head was coming from, some of them like paper cutouts, some frightening, some fascinating, all of them with a life of their own. Neither could I even presume to guess the source of the storm fronts that were blasting me, nor did I have any idea how to put a stop to the whole process. I still had a sense of a center, of a me, although it no longer seemed the self-evident and indestructible edifice that I had previously perceived it to be. That was because at one point I had found myself shrinking to microscopic proportions, and later my center, my ego, had come close to total disintegration as I started to expand macroscopically. I had been able to halt this expansion only by a fierce exertion of will power.

I spent much of the evening struggling to hold on to my self-control. As I continued to fight to maintain control, suddenly, with my eyes open, the wall adjacent to the bed on which I lay began to whisper. This was truly terrifying, for I was no longer merely viewing my own internal imagery, my own thought processes, this was an actual hallucination, entirely outside the powers of my own mind. I thought of madness, and I knew that this really was what others call madness. To me, though, it was mostly just frightening—I did not really feel mad, in the grips of lunacy, per se, just in chaos. But I did realize, I did assert to myself, that my will power was everything, that the only thing preventing me from succumbing to madness was that will power.

The whispering grew louder. It increased from a few whispers to a cacophony of whispers, like hundreds of whispering lips erupting on the face of the wall, for now I could *see* the wall whispering, too. I could not make out what the wall was trying to say though, nor did I wish to; for I feared that were I to actually discern the message, it would release a veritable floodtide of madness into a world that was already overwhelmingly chaotic. Yet, in spite of my resistance the message was starting to come through. I knew I must not listen to it. In desperation I tried to think of a song to block it out. The most effective song I could think of was the opening phrase from the Mozart 3rd Horn Concerto. I sang this phrase over and over until it was all that existed, until it literally drowned out the whispering voices. Every so often I stopped and listened to see if the voices were still there, and after awhile, mercifully, they subsided and were gone.

This phase of the evening's pyrotechnics had reached a fever pitch. The power of the storms had

increased, and the sky inside had gone totally wild. All
became dark, the heavens crackled; I felt my teeth shattering, then there was one deafening thunderclap and
like a glass figure inside which the pressure had become
too great, I exploded, shattering into a thousand shards
of glass that splintered up, up, up, and then floated noise-
lessly down like soft crystal snowflakes into the silence of
blissful unconsciousness. When I came to momentarily, I
found myself in an unbelievable state. I lay dismembered
on the bed: my head was off, lying above my right shoulder; my legs were severed from the trunk and lay to the
side of where they should be; my left arm was off too; my
right arm, though, was in the socket where it belonged
and I could move it. It was comforting to be able to hold
this arm tightly against my body. I hugged it the way a
child hugs its blanket. My intelligence was intact, which
meant that I knew where I was, I had my bearings about
me—in fact, I could have recited my life's history had it
been required of me, and I was not delusional. Still, there
was an inherent contradiction in my condition—I sensed
my limbs as having been, in effect, amputated, yet, the
reality was that they were still connected to my body. In
retrospect, thinking back to that moment, it doesn't seem
too farfetched to suppose that in addition to muscular,
skeletal, cartilaginous structures and tissues, the body's
appendages may be attached also by some sort of electro-
physical sheath of which medical science has no knowledge. Perhaps these kinds of limbs have connections that
can be disconnected without affecting the physical limbs.
At that moment, though, I would not have engaged in
such speculation, for it did not seem so illogical to be dismembered like that. Even so, this condition was exceedingly painful, and I just wanted to be whole again.
Blessedly the easy-listening music of WPAT was still
playing and this continued to soothe me. I curled into a

fetal position against my good arm, listened to the soft music, and waited it out. Gradually my head and limbs became reattached to my torso somehow, and I returned to normal.

I was deeply grateful to find myself in one piece again, but with my body's return to normalcy came a return of the storms. They were not as bad though, more like distant thunder now. As the storms lessened, I gradually became aware of an immense figure, similar to a picture frame, on the periphery of my visual plane. It was more rectangular than square or round, and it ran lengthwise from top to bottom. The rectangle was fairly plain, a deep brownish color, resembling a dark, golden, mahogany 17th-century picture frame. It was the kind of frame that could have contained a Rembrandt, except that no ornaments or images had been carved into it, and it was vibrating around its entire circumference. The rectangle, in fact, seemed to exist both inside and outside me at the same time. At various places around the edges, there were misshapen areas. The storms that were shaking me were simultaneously wrenching these misshapen areas, causing the entire rectangle to shake and quiver, and now I could see that the storms were having a positive effect, for after each storm occurred on the rectangle, the misshapen area that had been wrenched by the storm resumed its proper shape. Gradually, then, the entire surface was being restored to a perfectly symmetric rectangle. In the lulls between wrenchings, I began to feel, at last, a sense of peace and well-being, and it struck me that I was undergoing some sort of healing process, that by going through the storms I was becoming divested of traumatic knots that had built up over the course of my life. Healing or not, the internal sky began to darken as before, and the storms began rumbling with increasing frequency out over the darker plains of my consciousness. I began to fear that I might have to go through the entire experience all over.

With dread and alarm I watched the storms again building on the horizon. I doubted that I could endure a replay of what I had been through, yet even at that moment a new storm was already beginning to shake me. I felt as though I were lying on a narrow ledge that was beginning to crumble. Underneath this ledge lay an abyss and the unknown terrors of oblivion; all that kept the ledge from falling to pieces was my own strength, my own resolve. Now as that strength gave out, I could only cling to the ledge and pray that somehow I might summon even greater reserves of will power. It was as though I held the ledge together only by sheer determination, yet slowly, in spite of my struggles, the ledge was disintegrating beneath me, little by little, moment by moment. My grip was relaxing, my concentration was weakening, I could not hold on. Then finally, exhausted beyond endurance, I let go entirely, feeling at that precise moment that I had lost the battle for my very soul. But to my utter amazement, instead of spinning off into outer darkness as I had expected, I was greeted by a most pleasant sensation. For there was a sudden rush of energy up my spine! It felt almost electric, like a soothing current; it was, in fact, as I have since come to understand, the bioelectric energy called kundalini. The rush of energy felt extremely good. It startled me though and caused me to immediately grab hold again. Yet, intrinsically I knew that something remarkable had happened, something that signified more than just momentary relief from the nightmare I was caught in. I was still in danger, but now it seemed possible that the rushing energy might augur a way out of this seemingly inextricable situation.

I berated myself for tensing up, for grabbing hold again. Perhaps I had lost my chance; perhaps this curious energy would not rush up my spine again. I hardly dared think that this could be an avenue of escape, yet there might be no other way. I had felt the rush not only physically, but psychically as well. That is, not only had I felt it, but I had seen it internally, too. It looked similar to the double helix of the DNA molecule, was tinged with a bluish, yellowish, reddish-orange luminosity, and spiralled upward like a whirling gyroscope. I resolved that if the rush started up again I would not resist it. All night long, in trying to save myself, I had resorted exclusively to techniques of holding on, of resistance, of struggle. Now I had reason to suspect that the way to salvation lay through surrender, not through resistance, for the rush up my spine had begun at the exact moment of my surrender to the abyss. Already I could feel the storms building again in the distance. Perhaps this would be the final assault, perhaps I would not survive this time. How could I get the kundalini to come back? I sensed that the proper technique was to attend to it, yet at the same time, not really to attend to it, but to let it just happen. It was important not to try to dictate its activity, or movement; the idea was to pay attention to it, but in a discreet way, so that it could flow of its own accord. The situation required immediate action for a new storm was beginning to shake me again.

Suddenly, once again, I felt the little rush down toward the lower part of my back. With some misgiving, but nevertheless realizing it was my only hope, I gave up all resistance, and surrendered unconditionally to whatever fate awaited me. I did not know if I would go slithering off into outer space, or if I would be carried to safety by the kundalini energy. Either fate was acceptable at that moment, for I no longer had the strength to resist—I was totally exhausted. What did follow, however, was extraordinary. For the rush, the kundalini, no longer restrained, then rose swiftly, spiralling and whirling upward, gyroscoping up without impediment, up, up, and up, expanding, expanding, expanding consciousness as it rose, continuing up the length of my spine and finally right out through the top of my head in an explosion of consciousness. The feeling was blissful beyond description, and suddenly, just like that, I was propelled to another state of consciousness altogether. I found myself united, in a state of union, of oneness, with the universal consciousness, or intelligence, which is to say, with God. By this I do not mean a personal God—the sense one might have of God while praying or worshipping. Rather, what I experienced was a direct connection to the core of my being, through which flowed the creative power of the universe—as if I had suddenly become plugged in to the source of all creation. And the essence of this power, this autonomous power, I was discovering, was benevolence and love. With tears of joy and gratitude running down my cheeks, I found myself saying simply, "Ahhh!"

Soon I was struck by the realization: "This is who I really am!!!" For this was the real me. This was a new self, a complete self who superseded the old, shrunken, and only *partial* self I had previously perceived myself to be. For to be truly in touch with one's inner self, is not only to touch bliss, it is also to become a full person. Instinctively, I knew that my present state of consciousness, that which I later learned had been given the name *cosmic consciousness* by others who knew of it, was the birthright of every single human being. I realized that this throbbing, pulsating, glorious consciousness was the plane which had served as the basis for the world's religions and philosophies—this was the coveted philosopher's stone, this was the Buddha's nirvana, this was the Zen adept's satori, and here on this plane, will birth be given to the coming new age consciousness. I now knew what was "the peace that passeth understanding" of the Bible and how the psalmist of this same book had been able to say, "O Death, Where is thy Sting?" For to be in touch with this state of mind is to be in touch with one's core, which is all-pervading consciousness, or God. There is no death, for one *is* in one's essence God, and death itself no longer seemed frightening—indeed, for as long as I remained in that state of cosmic consciousness, I found it laughable that I had ever been afraid of it.

Eventually I went in search of my friend. The apartment was no longer ominous and foreboding. The music playing on the radio was pulsating, throbbing, and glorious. Objects in the room were radiant and vibrant in their colors, their very existence was a song to the joy of life. I was thrilled through and through, and I was truly grateful for the wonder of being alive.

I found my friend in the living room. He was now feeling better, too, and moving around. He stated that he felt as though he had died during the night. As nearly as one could tell, though, he had not awakened the kundalini energy. As we talked over the events of the evening, I found myself summarizing the new sense of myself, the newly acquired consciousness coursing through my brain, with the wondering statement, "This is intelligence!"

I did not remain long in that kingdom of the self into which I so miraculously floundered for just a few hours that night, though the phenomenal world around me did sometimes sparkle with a reminiscent lustre for the next two years. Yet, I was forever changed by the experience. For kundalini is a great psychic cleanser. As a result, certain self-doubts were forever erased and I gained a sense of self-confidence I had not previously possessed. And that is still with me today, some thirty years later. I have never had a resurgence of kundalini, which is to be expected. I did, after all, use a hallucinogen to jump-start my spiritual development that night, and I know that I will be able to reactivate the kundalini only after I have truly reached sufficient spiritual maturity. Nevertheless, moments do occur when I touch that immensity of which Krishnamurti always spoke, when I find that the everyday concerns of the self have unexpectedly diminished, and the marvelous environment spreads out all around me, soft and enchanting, encompassing me in the pulsating energy of silence.

• • • • •

In the preceding descriptions, kundalini was portrayed as an extremely potent and severe psychic force. Kundalini, however, may also manifest in a much gentler manner. Generally, the quality of kundalini awakening will be affected by one's physical and mental health. Mental outlook, in particular, may determine the quality of the experience more than any other factor. If one has an essentially laid-back attitude, certain internal dynamics, such as storms or hallucinations, may not appear so threatening; but if one has a tendency toward paranoia to start with, that may be magnified. One may rest assured, in any case, that where imbalance does exist in the mind or body, the kundalini energy is fundamentally geared toward restoration of health. This was demonstrated in all of the kundalini narratives. Of the four accounts, Dr. Motoyama may have been better equipped to cope, though the challenges he faced were no less formidable, for as he stated, his Brahman Gate was already open, making him perhaps better prepared for this kind of experience at the outset. With regard to benign kundalini awakenings then, it could be stated as a maxim that a healthy body and mind are prerequisite; and, such awakenings do occur, as will be discussed later in this text.

Here I should point out that although terms like *kundalini activation, kundalini arousal*, or *kundalini awakening* are used to describe this phenomenon, in actuality, kundalini is always active in the body. It is, in fact, as has been stated and as will be explored in greater depth in chapter 8, the veritable life force (prana) itself. Usually, however, the kundalini, or prana, operates at such a low frequency that one is not aware of it. Terms like *awakened* merely refer to a highly increased activation, in which the kundalini is brought demonstrably to an individual's attention.

Up to this point, we have seen how kundalini was described in the Tantras and some ways in which it is experienced today. Using all four of the preceding portraits to construct a paradigm, we may infer that kundalini is a *process* that starts when the prana in the body becomes more energized than usual. This process, when the experience is benign, may be characterized by heightened awareness and perception, internal imagery that is pleasant, joyful, even rhapsodic, followed by steps three and four below. When the process is difficult, it will usually be distinguished from beginning to end by at least one, sometimes all, of the symptoms in each of the following four categories sequentially:

1. **Dramatic Incipient Symptoms,** such as a painful lump on the nape of the neck; fever, trembling, burning sensations; vivid internal imagery; severe pain in the head and/or spine, or powerful energy rushing through the spine; great anxiety; the experience of visions, of hearing and/or seeing invisible presences, of being out of one's body, or of the body disintegrating.

2. **Period of adjustment with a Continuation of Incipient Symptoms,** marked by extreme heat, sensations of flames and of being literally burned; continued internal imagery, visions, both auditory and visual, great anxiety;

dramatic inner storms in which past traumas may be met head on, vented, and healed; seeing lights; perception of the immediate environment as dirty, filthy, untouchable, or the feeling that people are unclean and untouchable; disintegration, evidenced by a sense of expansion or contraction of the body, or by a feeling that the body has literally disintegrated or has fallen apart; continued out-of-body experiences and pain or energy rushing through the spine or head.

3. **Dramatic Climax.** This is the actual kundalini experience. It is the moment when there is a sensation of an internal current streaking like lightning up the spine in an explosion of transcendent consciousness and bliss. This marks the culmination—the epiphany—of the kundalini experience. This is the moment when all crises pass, when any fever is broken. It is the moment of rebirth, and transcendence and illumination follow.

4. **Transformed Personality** with benign, flowing kundalini—sometimes short-lived, sometimes permanent; internal imagery, visions, both auditory and visual, exaltation, great joy, altered perception of the phenomenal world as lustrous, marvelous, thrilling; psychic abilities; increased mental aptitude, even genius.

By now I hope a clear picture of kundalini is starting to emerge. In the following chapters, we will continue this investigation, first at the site of the chakras, to try to see whether they really exist or whether they are just a fanciful notion carried over from ancient religious superstitions. Then we will analyze kundalini in the context of madness and look at some historical evidence illustrating that in the past kundalini was known not only in India, but to many cultures and civilizations of the world. We will then return to our theme of madness, this time inquiring whether there is any common ground between kundalini and schizophrenia. Following this we will look into the thought of Gopi Krishna, who has articulated the biological basis of the mystical process like none before him, and we will take a brief look at the role hallucinogens have played in altered states of consciousness. I have then included two interviews with Gopi Krishna so that we may have more direct access to his experience through the process of dialogue. Finally, in the epilogue, we will consider what relevance kundalini has to the coming new age.

Chapter 4

Do The Chakras
Really Exist?

The Tantras depict nine chakras positioned along the spine. Seven are considered major, and two are minor. Figure 1 on page 6 shows these chakras as they are depicted in the Tantric texts. One is never quite certain, however, how to take these descriptions. Just when it appears that a symbol is allegorical, there is the perception that it was meant to be taken literally, that it casts shadows of real presences. A glimpse of the Goddess Kundalini leaping between the worlds of the seen and unseen, makes one wonder about one's notions of reality.

The chakras serve as centers for the manifestation of various human emotions such as love, fear, anger, and joy. They can be seen as different theatres, on the stages of which are portrayed an infinite variety of dramas, from fearful dungeon and dragon encounters in the nether-worlds to quantum leaps into the outer dimensions of the future. Chakras have been described as nerve centers governing the various organs, or as turning wheels, or vortices serving to connect the physical body to the etheric, astral, mental, or causal bodies.[1]

Chakras also function in a practical context. It is said that what we experience in our lives depends to a certain degree upon the chakra to which we are attuned, for each chakra is energized by certain emotional, mental, psychic, and spiritual attributes. Those who are in touch with the lower chakras will be more inclined to find and seek fulfillment through gratification of the physical senses, and those who have opened the gateways to the higher chakras will aspire toward intellectual and spiritual attainments. According to this view all people are in touch to some degree with the chakras, and their intellectual, artistic, and vocational capacities are directly influenced by the chakras to which they are most directly connected.

Chakras, then, can be viewed as energy centers, and much more; they can also represent access to other worlds, to other dimensions. As such, volumes could be written about each one. What follows is a brief description of the Tantric conception of the chakra complex. Though the Tantric models are on the surface allegorical and symbolic, it is well to remember that the Tantric tradition is suggestive of psychic realms. Seen in this light, the chakras may also be thought of as entranceways to the world of the paranormal, where healing, extrasensory perception, and precognition are indigenous features of the landscape.

In Tantrism, the chakras are depicted as lotus blossoms and as domains inhabited by Gods and Goddesses. The four elements—Earth, Water, Fire, Air—and basic sounds, smells, and sights are associated with the chakras, as well as the five senses. Thus, an experience of the Manipura chakra, for example, might include a vision of a ten-petalled lotus flower, an encounter with a fire-carrying God, increased acuity of sight, and the sound *ram* in the inner ear. Some hold that the Tantric chakras are real; others say they are allegorical. Whether or not these chakras and their deities and realms are real or allegorical, it is well worthwhile to spend some time traveling through them. By comparing the old to the new, it may be possible to determine which premise will stand the test of time and which one will not. Here then are the chakras as described in the texts of Tantrism.

1) **The Muladhara Chakra**— This is the lowest in the hierarchy of nine major and two minor chakras, and it is located at the base of the spine in the perineal region. Like all the chakras, sanskrit letters are inscribed on each petal, representing the different sounds of spiritual energy to which the chakra responds. In the very center is the letter most characteristic of the "sound" of the chakra, arising from all the energies which have converged in the chakra. In the Muladhara, that letter, or sound, is *lam*, and those who hear this sound internally, may know that they are in touch with the Muladhara chakra. It is in this chakra that the serpent force, the Devi Kundalini, lies dormant. The Devi has the lustre of lightning, and her tail is coiled 3½ times around a linga (symbol of Shiva) of molten gold. The first of three *Granthi Knots* is found in this chakra. A Granthi Knot is a dense cluster of *Maya Shakti* (maya meaning illusion, shakti meaning force, or power). Therefore, Maya Shakta could be called an *impasse contrived from the power of illusion.* (Passage must be gained through these Granthi Knots in order to progress to higher levels in the chakra complex.) The Muladhara chakra is also the site of Shabdabrahman, which means God (Brahman) as sound (Shabda). On the physical plane, Shabdabrahman manifests as kundalini. The Muladhara chakra has four crimson lotus petals and is

presided over by the four-armed Devi Dakini with brilliant red eyes, who is "the carrier of the revelation of the ever-pure intelligence," and the Deva Brahma, who is Lord of the physical world. This chakra may be called the chakra of physical experience. It is associated with the earth and the sense of smell.

2) **The Svadhisthana Chakra—**
This chakra has six vermilion lotus petals and is located below the navel in the area above the genitals. It is presided over by the blue lotus-colored Devi Rakini, of furious aspect, who carries weapons in her uplifted arms and the four-armed, luminous, blue Deva Vishnu, the all-pervading life-force of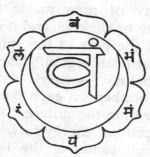
the universe. The sound of the Svadhisthana is *vam*. This chakra, like the Muladhara chakra, is closely allied with the earth. It is associated with water and the sense of taste.

3) **The Manipura Chakra—**This chakra has ten lotus petals the color of heavy rain clouds and is located at the solar plexus. It is presided over by the three-faced, three-eyed, four-armed, fire-carrying Devi Lakini, and her consort, the Deva Rudra, who is red in color, also four-armed and
fire-carrying, and who represents the world of mind. The sound of the Manipura is *ram*. Although Lakini is a meat-eater with denser attributes than a vegetarian, this chakra

is less earth oriented than the Muladhara and Svadisthana chakras, and could be regarded as more of an emotional center. The Manipura chakra is associated with fire
and the sense of sight.

4) **The Anahata Chakra**—This
chakra has twelve red lotus
petals and is located in the region
of the heart. It is presided over by
the Devi Dakini, who is three-
eyed, happy, and the benefac-
tress of everyone. The presiding
Deva Isha is also overlord of the
first three chakras; he is compas-
sionate and represents the revelation of the mysteries of
time and space. The second of the three Granthi Knots is
found in this chakra. The Anahata chakra may be regarded as a consciousness center, and it is here that the
sound can be heard which comes without the striking of
any two things together. This chakra is associated with air
and the sense of touch. The sound of the anahata is *yam*.

A. The Ananda-Kanda Chakra—This is one of the two
minor chakras. It is small, located just below the heart
(Anahata) chakra, and is often not cited. It does exist,
however, and has eight rose-red lotus petals. This chakra
is said to sometimes grant wishes even before they are
formulated in the mind.

5) **The Vissudha Chakra**—This chakra has sixteen smoky
purple lotus petals and is located in the region of the
throat. It is presided over by the Devi Shakini and the
Deva Sada-Shiva. Each is five-faced, three-eyed, and has
multiple arms. Shakini is shown in shining white, having

the form of light itself, and Sada-Shiva is an androgyne whose body is half white, representing Shiva, and half gold, representing Shakti. The sound of the Vissudha is *ham*. This chakra is connected with the purification of intelligence and is associated with ether and the sense of hearing.

B. **The Lalana Chakra**—This is the other minor chakra. It has twelve red lotus petals and is located above the throat (Vissudha) chakra at the root of the palate. It is associated with faith, contentment, a sense of error, self-command, anger, affection, purity, detachment, agitation, and appetite.

6) **The Ajna Chakra**—This chakra has two white lotus petals and is located between the eyebrows. This is a very small chakra, and its two petals just fill the space between the eyebrows. It is sometimes regarded as the mystical third eye—the inner or mental eye. The sound of the Ajna is *om*. The Ajna chakra is presided over by the Devi Hakini and her consort, the Deva Paramashiva, both of whom have entered a state of elation brought on by draughts of ambrosia. These deities are six-faced, three-eyed, with multiple arms, and shine like lightning. The third of the three Granthi Knots is found in this chakra. The Ajna Chakra is associated with mind and with mental faculties.

7) **The Sahasrara Chakra**—This chakra is called the *Lotus of One Thousand Petals*; upon its petals all colors are

combined, and it encompasses all sounds. It is located in the crown of the head. One could say it is presided over by the one Brahman, for here is where Kundalini-Shakti and Shiva will meet, reconnecting the Shiva-Shakti Tattva so that it is once again one with Brahman. The effulgence of a thousand lotus petals is the expression of enlighten- 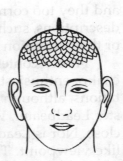 ment. The Sahasrara chakra, then, is synonymous with samadhi, and it is here that the explosion into cosmic consciousness occurs.

Perhaps a good place to begin a discussion of whether the chakras are real is with an important consideration: Who has drawn up the theory about them? The Tantric theory just discussed dates all the way back to the rishis, or seers, of ancient India. One would expect the high priests of such an arcane creed to have access to privi-leged, inside information—in this case, the direct experi-ence of kundalini and the chakras. And in certain respects, these ancient adepts do live up to such an expectation. For their 2000-year-old descriptions of Shiva, Shakti, and Kundalini-Shakti correspond closely to accounts of risen kundalini as it has occurred in other cul-tures, in other epochs, and even as it is reported today. The age old Tantric depiction of the kundalini energy as a serpent lying coiled and then rising hissing up the spine so closely parallels the bioelectric kind of energy that Gopi Krishna, Krishnamurti, Dr. Motoyama, and I described, in fact, that serious credence must be given to the purveyors of the serpent myth. Obviously there was real knowledge behind the allegory. The same kind of correspondences can be found in the Tantric chakras. They too have been perceived in other times and places, and they too correlate in some respects to contemporary descriptions, such as their location on the spinal channels or the perception of them as kundalini activated centers.

From a contemporary standpoint, probably very few chakra enthusiasts actually endorse the Tantric representations, although the etheric conception of Charles Webster Leadbeater, which has a wide following, does stray close. Nor is Leadbeater the only proponent of a Tantra-like viewpoint. The etheric, or nonphysical conception, which portrays the chakras as energy centers connecting physical, etheric, astral, mental, or causal, realms, is probably the most prevalent theory existing today. There is also the biological conception, which characterizes the chakras as actual physical organs of the body. In the four kundalini narratives, Gopi Krishna stated the biological position, and Dr. Motoyama reflected the etheric position. Krishnamurti did not take a position, and beyond a passing reference attributed to him by Pupul Jayakar where he remarked that the wheels are turning, was silent on the subject in his talks and books. I myself did not take a position either, for I had no perception of actual chakras. In the following section, I will state Gopi Krishna's position first, which both refutes the Tantric conception and illustrates the biological conception at the same time. After this I will present the etheric position as represented by Dr. Motoyama. Then I will analyze the viewpoint of Charles Webster Leadbeater, whose book *The Chakras* presents a conception that resembles in many respects the chakras of Tantrism.[2] By comparing these three differing views, perhaps we will come closer to the answer to our question: Do the chakras really exist?

According to Gopi Krishna's analysis in *The Secret of Yoga*, the Tantric descriptions do not correspond to reality, nor is it reasonable to ask people living in the present century to take such representations seriously. He says, ". . . it is not difficult to imagine how impossible it is for a modern informed mind to reconcile the descriptions of the ancient masters . . . with the characteristics of the cerebrospinal system contained in modern texts on physiology."[3] Seen through Gopi Krishna's eyes, it is easy to see, nevertheless, how the ancient viewpoint evolved. He writes:

> Considering the general ignorance concerning the basic facts of physiology prevailing during the past, and the superstitious awe with which the inexplicable phenomena relating to the mind and body were regarded, even by the intelligent and learned in ancient times, it is not surprising that the ancient masters created a whole host of divinities and strange formations in the body to account for the bewildering effects caused by *kundalini*.[4]

What is now necessary is to "elucidate and reconcile the . . . fantastic and impossible assertions about the lotuses and the cakras"[5] with present-day scientific knowledge.

Gopi Krishna is not saying, however, that the chakras do not exist, but merely that the Tantric conception is not realistic. He goes on to state that seen without superstition or preconceived ideas, the chakras actually are "concentrations of nerves having a circular formation"; they are "thick clusters of intersecting nerves."[6] The psychic force experienced on the awakening of kundalini is felt in these nerve clusters (chakras) and the movement is circulatory, giving the impression of a wheel turning. This would account for Krishnamurti's perception of turning wheels. Moreover, Gopi Krishna's view is not merely theoretical, for in another text continuing his argument against the concept of chakras as lotuses, he writes, ". . . if I had [practiced Tantric methods] with a firm belief in the existence of the lotuses, I might well have mistaken the luminous formations and the glowing discs of light at the various nerve junctions along the spinal cord for lotuses. . . ."[7] In other words, Gopi Krishna actually could see the chakras.

Gopi Krishna believed, in fact, that all the kundalini processes could be seen and are physical, including the nerves called *Nadis*. He states that the view expressed by Arthur Avalon, the author of *The Serpent Power* and other important books on kundalini, "that *Nadis* are subtle channels of pranic or vital energy is not thus borne out by the statements contained in the ancient treatises."[8] (The term *subtle channels*, of course, refers to nonphysical, or etheric channels.) Gopi Krishna asserts that due to this misinterpretation of the ancient texts, the misconception has arisen that the energy channels are not physical. "Once it is admitted that the term *Nadis* used by ancient writers refers to nerves present in our flesh and blood, there should come a change in the concept of Kundalini-Yoga, and the doctrine . . . should touch the solid surface of earth as a verifiable biological phenomenon."[9]

Gopi Krishna supports this argument with quotations from the Upanishads, proving that the ancient mystics did not state that the nadis had a nonphysical existence. The confusion that has arisen about their essential quality, he says, has occurred because they are so very fine—they are invisible, in fact, to the naked eye. This also explains why they are still unknown to science. Gopi Krishna states that these "nerve fibrils are as fine as the thousandth part of a hair," and writes that Pancastavi in verse 2 of the Brhadaranyaka-Upanishad "likens *kundalini* to the fine filament of the maidenhair fern, a very apt illustration for the slender nerve-fibers covering the human body."[10]

To further illustrate his point, Gopi Krishna notes that if the writer of the Tantras had been referring to non-physical energy channels rather than to actual nerves, then

> instead of suggesting the arduous and even dangerous practice of *pranayama*, which directly affects both the autonomic and the central nervous system, combined with postures, *mudras* and *bandhas* that are unequivocally physical exercises, the ancient masters would have contented themselves with recommending purely mental exercises. . . . That from prehistoric times complicated, laborious, and painful psychosomatic methods have been used provides unmistakable evidence that the mechanism to be stimulated has an objective and concrete reality. . . .[11]

In his writings, Gopi Krishna emphasizes the biological infrastructure of the kundalini process at every opportunity. He asserts and reasserts that the chakras are physical and that the entire process—prana, kundalini, nadis, and the chakras—may be visually perceived (through the mind's eye) and will one day be verified by science. This scientific verification is the distinguishing mark of Gopi Krishna's approach. He constantly stresses the importance of arriving at a critical, objective appraisal of the chakras and of the kundalini process. Gopi Krishna writes, "Uncritical acceptance of the existing accounts . . . has made the subject more obscure and complicated and resulted in lending currency to false and misleading notions about this mighty power. The extent to which even the learned have been carried away by the cryptographic descriptions and cabalistic signs and diagrams is surprising. . . ."[12] In sum, Gopi Krishna's arguments are persuasive, and his conviction that the chakras are biological realities cannot be dismissed lightly.

Gopi Krishna's argument helps validate the descriptions of the chakras given by Dr. Motoyama. For it does not seem too preposterous in respect of the points Gopi Krishna makes to state that just as electricity can be seen under the right conditions—for instance when lightning strikes—and just as kundalini itself can be seen under the right conditions (in the four kundalini narratives the kundalini was seen internally), so too can the chakras be seen when the right conditions prevail, as Dr. Motoyama has testified. At this juncture, then, the focus of our question shifts from whether the chakras actually exist to: whether their existence is physical, as Gopi Krishna has asserted; or whether they are the kinds of nonphysical chakras affirmed by Dr. Motoyama and Charles Webster Leadbeater. Let us look at Dr. Motoyama's chakras next.

Dr. Motoyama depicted the chakras as a "blackish-red light like a ball of fire"[13] in his lower abdomen, a "round, crimson fire ball"[14] in his abdomen, a "reddish light centered on the navel,"[15] or a golden light shining from his heart. At the close of *Theories of the Chakras*, Dr. Motoyama summarizes his views about these colored lights and fireballs. He writes:

> **A.** The chakras are the centers of the body's energy systems, which exist in each of the three different dimensions, physical, astral, and causal.

> **B.** Each chakra has three levels, and each level of the chakra functions in the corresponding dimension. These functions, however, are closely related to each other.

C. The chakras act as intermediaries between the three dimensions, and can convert the energy of one dimension into that of another.[16]

Thus, Dr. Motoyama has taken a position more in keeping with the etheric viewpoint of the chakras.

From the preceding, it may be seen that the differences between the biological and the etheric positions cannot be resolved at this time. Since the chakras are invisible, and since no hard proof is available, precedence cannot be granted to either Gopi Krishna's or Dr. Motoyama's ideas. What is now required is conclusive scientific data about the exact makeup and precise location of the chakras. To this end Dr. Motoyama has been conducting scientific testing and research designed to measure these unseen processes in the body. I do not know whether Dr. Motoyama's experiments address the issues Gopi Krishna has raised as well as his own field of inquiry. But both sides of the issue seem worth investigating and hopefully parapsychology will begin to embrace all sides of this question in future research.

In this century the ideas of the theosophist Charles Webster Leadbeater probably have been the most influential in sustaining the etheric chakra theory. I believe that Leadbeater's theories have a serious credibility problem, nonetheless, even though his ideas seemingly dominate the field. His book, *The Chakras*, is still readily available; his works are still published by Quest Books, the publishing house of the Theosophical Society, which lists twenty-eight Leadbeater titles in its catalogue; and his theories are still given serious consideration in discussions about chakras. Indicative of Leadbeater's standing is the entire chapter devoted to his conception of the chakras in Motoyama's book, *Theories of the Chakras*. Motoyama closes this chapter with an encomium to Leadbeater's pioneering work describing the etheric centers as he perceived them. Dr. Motoyama does feel constrained to admit later, however, when he begins to describe the chakras as he himself experienced them, that he has a problem "with Leadbeater's assertion that the chakras he experienced were the true ones...."[17]

Leadbeater's ideas on the chakras were derived from theosophy, Yoga, and presumably his own clairvoyant insights. Briefly, he holds that the chakras are etheric centers connected with certain ganglia in the body. Each chakra is an energy vortex, perpetually rotating, and into each chakra a seven-fold primary force from the higher world is always flowing. The chakras appear as small circles about two inches in diameter when undeveloped, but "when awakened and vivified they are seen as blazing, coruscating whirlpools, much increased in size, and resembling miniature suns."[18] The primary force radiates from the hub of the vortex in a manner to form an exact number of spokes in each chakra, and these in turn, determine the number of undulations (waves or petals, for they resemble flowers) in the chakra. Each chakra has an exact number of spokes. The brow chakra has 96 spokes, for example, the crown chakra has 960, and so on.

These chakras are etheric and correspond with a set of astral chakras. The function of the etheric chakras is to "bring down into physical consciousness whatever may be the quality inherent in the astral centre which corresponds to it."[19] Thus, there are two sets of chakras in Leadbeater's system. Kundalini, which he calls the serpent-fire, resides in the first chakra in each of the systems. The chakras vary in size and color as do the Tantric chakras, and generally, could be described as the Leadbeater variations on a Tantric theme. Leadbeater is creative, and there is no limit to the spin he is able to apply to Tantra. For instance, in the Leadbeater system, prana, which he renames "vitality," originates in the sun and then manifests in a globule to be drawn into the human body through the spleen chakra, where it is subdivided into seven vitality rays of differing colors. As Leadbeater describes the process, "These rays then pass off in different directions, each to do its special work in the vitalization of the body."[20] He goes on to say of the seven rays, "Vitality is thus clearly sevenfold in its constitution, but it flows through the body in five main streams."[21]

Here, as throughout *The Chakras*, it becomes increasingly difficult to come to terms with Leadbeater's advocacy of the symbolic, the magical, and the occult. The bulk of his system seems geared toward transmuting the Tantric formulations of the chakras and kundalini into an even more esoteric cosmology. One begins to ask, where are the proofs for these theories?

Previously we insisted that the rishis of old, the high priests of Tantric Yoga, know their subject intimately, that is, that they "spake" from firsthand knowledge of kundalini and the chakras. Ideas as influential as Leadbeater's in advancing the etheric chakra theory must surely be put to the same test, and perhaps the time has come to hold those ideas up to the serpent fire that Leadbeater espouses. For in *The Chakras*, Leadbeater has a great deal to say about kundalini. His kundalini writings are more or less consistent with Tantric theory, to be sure, and one finds nothing original except for an occasional theosophical twist at the end. This is a trifle disappointing, but is of no major consequence. When it comes to venturing beyond the theoretical to a description of personal experience of kundalini, however, which Leadbeater does attempt, he becomes significantly reticent. In a section titled "Personal Experience" [of kundalini], he writes only four very pallid, inconsequential paragraphs.

Here is the entire description of his own kundalini experience excerpted from the four paragraphs: ". . . one day one of the Masters" [one of the Theosophical Masters] "made a suggestion to me with regard to a certain kind of meditation which would evoke this force [kundalini]. Naturally I at once put the suggestion into practice, and in course of time was successful."[22]

That's it! Those two sentences are the sum total of what Leadbeater has to say about his own kundalini awakening. Considering how dramatic and powerful an activated kundalini can be, and how voluble most people are about the experience, this does seem curious. From a man who could fill a 609 page book titled *Science of the Sacraments*[23] with detailed information about the Vestments of the Church, Holy Orders, poetic descriptions about a pectoral cross, and various liturgical considerations, it seems even more peculiar. Leadbeater, very likely, could have been clairvoyant. He did, after all, discover Krishnamurti, if the Theosophical account is taken at face value, and Krishnamurti more than lived up to expectations. But did Leadbeater really have a personal experience of kundalini? There is not much evidence to suggest that he did, although he may have had *some*, albeit limited, personal experience, as illustrated in a letter written on May 12, 1923 to Annie Besant about Krishnamurti's "process."[24] In this letter he wrote that he didn't understand why Krishnamurti was undergoing so much suffering. He was particularly puzzled because Krishnamurti was a Brahmin, therefore of an especially pure heritage, and should not have been encountering those kinds of difficulties. He, himself, couldn't remember anything comparable when he went through this stage, although he stated that he did recall extreme discomfort as the kundalini began to develop. It could be, as Mrs. Besant had suggested to Leadbeater, that Krishnamurti's discomfort might simply be the preparation of his body for the coming of the Lord Maitreya. Leadbeater concluded that Krishnamurti's case was so unusual that all they could do was to bide their time and keep him under close observation.[25]

In other words, Leadbeater was conversant with kundalini, but when confronted with a profound case of kundalini awakening, he was clearly out of his depth. If he really understood kundalini, as he claimed, he would have grasped the full significance of Krishnamurti's symptoms immediately. Emily Lutyens pressed Leadbeater for some guidance about Krishnamurti's condition, and her account provides some insight into the kind of counsel that Leadbeater was able to offer Krishnamurti about kundalini. Lady Emily reported that Krishnamurti had been very desirous of discussing his process with Leadbeater, and they did meet several times to talk about this subject. Leadbeater, however, seemed loath to discuss the matter and was of little or no help. He informed Lady Emily that the process was beyond his experience and besides, that it had nothing to do with preparing Krishnamurti for the initiations. Leadbeater called it "the forcing of the spirillae in each atom." When Lady Emily insisted that Leadbeater explain himself, he replied that persons of the fifth root-race had a limited number of spirillae operating in the atoms of their brains; therefore, it was necessary that Krishnamurti, who apparently was only a fifth root-race man, have more spirillae opened. This would place him on a level with persons of the sixth root-race, and would prepare his body for the coming of the Lord Maitreya. Unfortunately, awakening these spirillae was a painful process, and this would account for Krishnamurti's extreme turmoil.[26]

Now, root races are a theosophical concept, and Leadbeater would understandably fall back upon such ideas in a crisis. But surely such musings gave Krishna-murti little solace. In retrospect, one can only feel sorry for the long-suffering Krishnamurti. For in the face of a heightened kundalini awakening in someone who was in serious trouble, Leadbeater had no relevant counsel to offer.

To conclude, it does not appear that Leadbeater had any great personal experience of kundalini, and if it is true that the chakras are awakened through the arousal of kundalini, as he unequivocally states in The Chakras, then it would seem that he had no great experience of the chakras either. Leadbeater writes, "This force [kun-dalini] exists on all planes, and by its activity the rest of the centers [chakras] are aroused."[27] Leadbeater is very definite about this, for a few pages later he restates this theme. ". . . to bring [the] first chakra into full activity is precisely to awaken the inner layers of the serpent fire. When once that is aroused, it is by its tremendous force that the other centers are vivified."[28] Therefore, Lead-beater's own chakras, by his own standards, were not "vivified," for he does not convince us that he himself has awakened the kundalini. Dr. Motoyama supports Leadbeater's thesis by writing that a chakra cannot be opened unless it has been activated by an awakened kundalini.[29] Motoyama's statement notwithstanding, it may be that an awakened kundalini is not a prerequisite for the opening of the chakras. It is entirely possible that they could be experienced merely as the result of height-ened prana. True or not, if Leadbeater was aware of such a possibility, he did not say so. It would follow, then, that the chakras he wrote about are merely theoretical. Lead-beater was a theoretician. His entire oeuvre demon-strates this. He loved charts and diagrams and complicated schematics and explanations—the more occult, the better. He wove a conception intricate and grand, but when the full tapestry is appraised, one feels uncertain as to its true value.

So, then, do the chakras exist? Hopefully the future will yield some bona fide scientific information to answer this question. As far as Leadbeater's theories are concerned, they remain to be substantiated. Gopi Krishna, on the other hand, has presented a system of ideas that he himself plucked from the serpent fire, and therefore, they are ideas worthy of serious consideration. When Dr. Motoyama speaks of the chakras, he is speaking from personal knowledge also, for it was the current of kundalini generated by his own meditation that set his chakras glowing. Therefor_, he too, must be taken seriously.

Without scientific validation, though, any statement about the chakras may be seen as no more than a superstitious belief still echoing from the Dark Ages. Gopi Krishna died in 1984, before the research projects he had planned could come to fruition. Fortunately, we do have the legacy of his writing and recorded talks and discussions. These can, at least, help point the way for future research. And, it seems likely that Dr. Motoyama will have some important contributions to make as he collects more data in his laboratory. There may be others now engaged in such projects, as well. At the present time, then, until the results of such tests come in, there appears to be no verifiable scientific answer to our question: Do the chakras really exist? But on an empirical level, as has been illustrated, there is ample evidence for contending that the chakras, either as biological or etheric/astral entities, do, in fact, actually exist.

My own viewpoint with regard to the chakras has not solidified. I have never seen a chakra, nor had I even heard of them at the time of my kundalini experience. What I understand of them is based on the Tantric formulations and the descriptions given by Gopi Krishna and Dr. Motoyama. Of greater interest to me than the chakras are the corollaries between Tantra and my own experience of kundalini. One of the most striking of these is that of a serpent uncoiling from its lair at the base of the spine. The serpent is without question the same bioelectric energy I felt running up my own spine. This particular allegory is what made Tantra interesting to me. All features of the Hindu description do not, of course, fall so neatly within the parameters of what I personally understand kundalini to be. For I did not have a sense of actual spinal chakras per se, rather, just of vast, internal realms.

Nevertheless, if I were to describe my own kundalini experience according to the Tantric conception of the chakras, I probably would begin by saying that the ominous hum I first heard in the bedroom issued from the Muladhara chakra. This is where Shabdabrahman dwells as the Devi Kundalini, and it is said, therefore, that in this chakra all sound is born. The Hindu model distinguishes between lettered Shabda, that is, sound with significance, like the sound of letters or words of language, and unlettered Shabda, that is, raw, un-differentiated, abstract sound. The hum I heard, then, was unlettered Shabda. I would then infer that my encounter with the raging fires occurred in the Manipura chakra, where the primary element is fire, and where the presiding deities Lakini and Rudra each carry fire in one of their four hands. Gopi Krishna affirms the connection of fire to this chakra, "of which the navel is the hub,"[30] when he writes, "It is universally accepted by the ancient writers that 'heat' resides in the umbilical center to carry out the function of digestion. It is, therefore, in accord with this idea to say that *kundalini* burns in the navel."[31] He then states that the sensation of a great fire reveals that kundalini has been activated in the umbilical region.

I might then conjecture that the episode in which I shattered like a glass figure took place in the Anahata, the heart chakra, which is located right above the Manipura chakra, and which houses the second of the fabled Granthi Knots—this under the presumption that the shattering was the result of difficulty in passing through the Granthi. I would conclude that the vibrating rectangle which appeared in my mind's eye shortly before my excursion into the transcendental plane, which is to say the Sahasrara chakra, may have actually been a chakra as it manifests as a visual image, perhaps the Vissudha, next in line above the Anahata, since it appeared after the shattering. I am postulating this only because the rectangle looked similar to some 18th and 19th century Rajasthani paintings of chakras featured in Ajit Mookerjee's book, *Kundalini: The Arousal of the Inner Energy*,[32] that I have seen since my kundalini experience. On the other hand the rectangle may have been the third of the Granthi Knots, which exists in the Ajna chakra. So my recollections would include passage through the Muladhara, Manipura, Anahata, either the Vissudha or Ajna, and the Sahasrara chakras. All this may have some basis in reality, but then again, it may not. I neither believe nor disbelieve in the chakras. But I always bear in mind the persuasive ideas of Gopi Krishna. I expect that he will be proven right eventually, and that one day the chakras will be recognized as actual organs of the central nervous system—as necessary to sustaining life and a well-balanced organism as are the glands and organs of the body we now know about, like the heart, liver, or the pituitary. To me, though, more important than all of this, than whether or not the chakras exist, is to keep one's eye on the prize, which is the transformation of consciousness that is possible through the awakening of kundalini.

For more than two millennia the chakras have stood the test of time as symbols of the mythological and the noumenal. Perhaps they are more than allegorical, perhaps they point to actual realities. Perhaps it is time to think of the noumenal in concrete terms—to dare to think that what is represented here may not be just fantasy, may not be just a dream, but on the contrary, may actually exist as another world, with different physical properties perhaps, but as real nevertheless, as the everyday physical world that all humanity acknowledges. That the chakras as symbols are so long lived suggests that they may represent a dimension that could be verified, and that may be worth serious investigation by the scientific community.

Chapter 5

The Downside of
Kundalini—Madness!

ll four kundalini narratives described symptoms one would expect to find in the case histories of asylum inmates. Gopi Krishna heard roaring sounds, and saw showers of light and satanic creatures leering at him at night. Added to that was the inability to focus his thoughts, the perception of a tongue of flame licking his organs, and a sense of fires raging like a furnace within. Krishnamurti's symptoms could have been equated with lunacy—the presence of mighty beings in his invisible world, the fierce pains in his head, the out-of-body experiences, the disintegration of personality leaving only an elemental part of consciousness remaining, or the walk that left bits and pieces of himself behind on the road. Dr. Motoyama tells of the sound of buzzing bees around his tailbone, of discs of light invisible to most other people, and he reports a confrontation with a demon. He describes a time when he stood paralyzed with fear at the edge of an abyss inside his own head and details out-of-body experiences and conversations with spirits. In my own account, I fled in terror from a crawling, undulating tapestry, and experienced flames burning inside myself. There were storms bursting in my head, and I heard and saw a wall whispering.

Finally my personality was totally shattered, and I ended up dismembered on a bed.

On the surface, it would appear that any one of these symptoms would have been enough to usher the four of us right into the inner sanctum of any institution in the Western world. For these are classic symptoms of mental disorder. And each of us were as disabled by our symptoms as any comparable patient in an asylum. Fortunately, we were able to remain in an environment where we were safe, remaining with those who loved and cared for us. But why is it that so many people with similar symptoms end up institutionalized and sedated?

Part of the answer may be found in general societal attitudes, for certain concepts about altered states of mind have been inculcated into us since childhood. We have been conditioned to believe that the world existing on the other side of consciousness is a world inhabited by howling demons and unchained anarchy; therefore, to cross that border, is to enter the kingdom of madness. Perhaps a certain madness, a certain anarchy, does exist on the other side of that border, as will be demonstrated in the following pages, but there are also spiritual and psychic realms that have yet to be adequately explained. The four kundalini accounts are representative of spiritual realms, obviously, but the theme of madness is present as well. Gopi Krishna thought that he had arrived at the border of madness "suspended by a thread, swinging . . . between sanity and insanity, between light and darkness, between heaven and earth."[1] Krishnamurti wrote, "I toss about, groan & moan and mutter strange things, in fact, almost behave like one possessed. . . . I may become clairvoyant when it is all over or . . . I am gradually going mad!!!"[2] I, too, thought of madness and I knew that this really was what others call madness. . . . I did assert to myself that my will power was everything, that the only thing preventing me from succumbing to madness was that will power.[3] Dr. Motoyama, while not mentioning the word *madness* itself, did describe a "dangerous stage"[4] in his practice and felt that he had become emotionally unstable.

It is no wonder that Gopi Krishna, Krishnamurti, Dr. Motoyama, and I all equated our symptoms with madness. Collectively, most people probably agree as to what comprises madness—hallucinations, certain erratic or inappropriate behaviors, paranoid delusions, going off into trance-like, catatonic states—all of these probably would fit rather neatly into the consensus view of psychosis. The case files of many patients showing these symptoms support the consensus viewpoint, as does the clinical assessment of what constitutes psychosis. We will look at this clinical view more fully in chapter 7 when the discussion centers on schizophrenia. But for now it can be said that it was not unreasonable that Gopi Krishna, Krishnamurti, Dr. Motoyama, and I thought we were going mad or becoming emotionally unstable—almost anyone else in a comparable situation would have come to the same conclusion.

The investigation that follows presents some examples of symptoms found in institutionalized patients that are similar to the states described in the four kundalini narratives. My purpose is to show the similarity of the symptoms in these narratives to those of psychosis and then to ask what actually constitutes madness, whether the kundalini narratives really depicted madness and why it is that of two people presenting the same symptoms, one ends up in a mental institution, and the other becomes an integrated, well-balanced, human being.

Some of the case files from which I have drawn data go all the way back to the early part of the century, to a time when the ideas of Sigmund Freud were making an impact upon psychiatry, and some are contemporary; but all of them are reminders of the pain, humiliation, defeat, and bewilderment that can descend upon someone whose mental underpinnings have gone awry. After studying these accounts for awhile, I began to feel like an intruder into another individual's most private secrets, as if I were an archaeologist digging up hallowed remains from a sacred tomb. I was struck with the importance of treating these histories with dignity and of reassuring these haunted materializations of my compassion, of our compassion, to invoke their indulgence, their understanding, their permission across the dimensions of time and space for this probe into a past that might be more happily forgotten. With all due respect, then, here are some of the patients' descriptions: ". . . last night I was laying there and somebody stood by and pushed me into the flames and I was burned. It was terrible. And I am still burning. . . ."[5] One patient complained, ". . . thoughts are so fleeting, as if cut off, connections are lost, thoughts are so rushed. . . ."[6] Another patient said, ". . . I feel absolutely muddled . . . I can't control my thoughts . . . they are confused. . . ."[7]

Many patients spoke of currents and electricity. The case file on one woman noted: ". . . Threads are being pulled out of her spine. . . . The current sends jerks through her body, especially through the sexual organs . . . it rips the flesh off her muscles, and it burns and smokes her leg."[8] A male patient said that "quantities of current" were influencing his body to "keep-it-alive."[9] A woman complained that "she was being hypnotically taught the most terrible things. Currents were being fed up her nose."[10] A man "spoke of the devil who harassed him and of voices and electric currents."[11] A female patient, the same woman who had been pushed into the flames, "insisted that the clothes in the locker were charged with electricity. "I am charged with electricity and can't get up,"[12] she informed her custodians. This same woman saw flashes of light. She was also delusional, accusing the hospital staff of poisoning her.

Hallucinations were common. Karl Jaspers, known as one of the originators of existentialist philosophy, and who was an M.D. practicing in psychiatry and teaching psychology at Heidelberg before his transition to philosophy, profiled some alcohol, hashish, and morphine experimentation in his first major book *General Psychopathology*, published in 1913. The intoxications produced in those studies are characterized as "model psychoses,"[13] as it were. Jaspers also included comparisons of mescaline and psychotic states in his text. In these mescaline studies, described as "a vivid analogy"[14] to some psychotic experiences, the experimenter, Serko, who himself ingested mescaline, tells what hallucinations look and feel like. He says:

> Haptic hallucinations sometimes fuse with visual ones in an odd way difficult to describe. In a vaguely illuminated visual field there form certain strips of light with a lively movement, turning into spirals which move to and fro in the visual field while rapidly rotating. There is at the same time a transformation in the haptic field whereby my leg assumes a spiral form too. The light spirals and the haptic spirals fuse together in consciousness so that the same spiral that is visually hallucinated is also perceived haptically . . . one feels a complete bodily and visual unity. . . .[15]

In actual "psychotic" states, patient hallucinations may include "faces staring in the window," "a ghostly face

88 • Darrel Irving

that gets bigger and smaller," "faces in the trees," "animals, faces, and larvae."[16] One woman "felt during the night that she was pulled suddenly by the hair at the back of the neck on the left, pulled with great force. At the same time, she saw a great flame flare up for a moment from the depths and then die down. She awoke immediately, and once awake there was nothing more to be seen, but she knew this had not been a dream. It had been real and it had wakened her."[17]

Let us now compare the patients' symptoms to the kundalini narratives given in chapter 3. It is obvious from the start, that the kinds of symptoms reported in the foregoing accounts are similar to those reported in the kundalini descriptions, for instance, the light spirals reported by Serko. These could be construed to be the chakras described by Krishnamurti or Motoyama as much as they could be taken to be the "weird circle of light and swirling luminous currents"[18] reported by Gopi Krishna. Generally, the similarity of the symptoms is quite striking. These first descriptions are especially like Gopi Krishna's experiences. The woman in the preceding paragraph reported a large tongue of flame rising from the depths. In Gopi Krishna's description, "a large tongue of flame would leap across his spine into his head,"[19] and he, too, like the patients above, spoke of a vital current, luminous currents, or a current flowing through his body. He too, was unable to focus his thoughts, unable to concentrate. He too, found himself in the midst of flames and burning.

From comparisons like these, there are not only dramatic similarities to be observed, but one begins to see right away an important difference between the patient and kundalini accounts—in the manner in which each group reacted to these powerful forces of the unconscious. Many of the patients, like the woman who was

certain the staff was trying to poison her, were delusional. They were thoroughly confused, disoriented,
were no longer certain of their identities, and required
help to return to a functional plane where they could
once again test reality for themselves. In the kundalini
accounts, on the other hand, no one became delusional,
no one lost their sense of themselves, and no one lost the
ability to test reality.

Generally, the kundalini narratives mirrored the
states of madness chronicled by the patients we are sur-
veying here. Take Krishnamurti, for example: his com-
munication with the masters and beings from other
planes, his clairvoyance; his sense of himself as one who
was God-intoxicated, as an emissary of the divine, "to
help the whole world climb a few feet higher";[20] the constant pain in his spine, the intense heat, the severe
headaches, the feeling that needles were being driven
into the top part of his head; and the bizarre behavior, "I
toss about, groan and moan and mutter strange things, in
fact almost behave like one possessed."[21] All of these
symptoms can be seen in the accounts that follow.

A woman entered a clinic complaining that she was
injured in her spine, that her back was knocking, and
that her head ached, ". . . with a smiling face [she stated
that] she was 'dead, although alive.' She claimed to have
a curious feeling in her head, a straining in the fingers, a
knocking in the back, a pulling in the eyes, and a shrinking in the brain. She claimed that there must be a knot in
her head and a cleft in her skull."[22] Another patient
reported, "With every word spoken to me or near me,
with every slight noise, I feel a blow on my head, producing a certain pain. The pain-cessation feels like an
intermittent pulling in my head, probably linked with a
rending of part of the skull-bone."[23] A female patient
told her doctor, "When I go to sleep I have the sensation

of everybody watching me. The pain in my head is terrible. I know when I talk to you I do funny things."[24] A woman complained that when "the radio was playing, she felt a heat in her head, as if from electricity."[25] Another woman "felt her body was being tortured by an external force. She said her spinal fluid was of course there still and her body did not have any punctures; she had only had these feelings."[26]

A man who was hallucinating explained that he could hear what other people were thinking. He entered an institution stating that he had the instructions of his father to save humanity. His moods were elevated, depending upon the degree of ecstasy, and he claimed that he was Jesus Christ. This period of institutionalization lasted about five months, after which he got married and raised a family. Twenty-eight years later, he was again institutionalized, speaking of the invention of an air ship, the pedigree of his poodle, and of the teachings of "Mazdazna,"[27] which he became preoccupied with. Another male patient who experienced elevated moods and ecstatic states, "claimed that his hands were full of rays, that he had divine power, and that he would establish a new religion."[28]

These accounts are remarkably similar to Krishnamurti's descriptions. The list could, of course, go on indefinitely. For instance, one could cite reports of unseen presences, like the woman who saw "spirits seated at a table," one of them was "a hermaphrodite with female appearance and male ability." Or the male patient who "sees spirits like ones in the movies and also sees God himself." There are more. A female patient informed her doctor that at night unseen "people come into the room and stand behind her."[29] A man noted "visual signs on the window and heard his wife and son talking" even though they were not present. He also "saw and heard angels, particularly the Archangel Michael."[30]

In view of our discussion in chapter 4 about chakras, it is interesting to see whether any of the patients reported visualizations of the kind that Dr. Motoyama reported. There were some, seemingly. One patient described a walk one evening. He was on a busy street and suddenly, momentarily, he felt nauseous. As he recovered, he perceived a small patch, about the size of a hand. It shimmered internally, and there was a back and forth movement of dark threads.[31] The woman who was previously described with currents running up her nose also claimed she could read thoughts and felt persecuted by a spotlight. "Do you hear that spot light? Now they have it on again."[32] Voices spoke to her from the ceiling and repeated whatever she was thinking. She continued to feel the spotlight and described a peculiar jerking in her arms and legs. The rotating spirals described by Serko, viewed in this context, may also correspond to Dr. Motoyama's chakras.

There were other symptoms reminiscent of Dr. Motoyama's accounts. A female patient reported that "doctors operating at a distance had removed her astral body and her brain and that her head was soft."[33] A male patient complained about voices and discovered to his surprise that he was able to have a conversation with his brother-in-law who lived elsewhere. He was able to do this by means of an inner voice. He also thought there "must be a radio or something"[34] through which someone was threatening and scolding him. He also heard his wife telling him that he should come home and that in his home town there had been a fire.

Demons were also seen. One woman who heard voices, "was in contact with spirits" and stated that the

Devil had "marked the Pope and the Emperor."[35] Here is a detailed account of demons:

> I felt as if I were continuously among criminals or devils. As soon as my strained attention wandered off from things around me, I saw and heard them, but I didn't always have the power to deflect my attention from them to other tangible objects. Every effort to do that was like rolling a millstone uphill. For instance, the attempt to listen to a friend's conversation that lasted more than a few sentences resulted in such restlessness (because these threatening figures towered over us) that I had to take my quick departure. It was extremely hard to attend [to] an object for any length of time. My thoughts would wander off at once to far-away places where demons would at once attack me, as if provoked. At first this shift of thought, this giving way, happened voluntarily and was sought by me, but now it happens on its own. It was a sort of weakness, I felt driven to it irresistibly. In the evening when trying to sleep I closed my eyes and would enter the vortex willy-nilly.[36]

This description reminds one of Motoyama's experience in the Vissudha chakra where he found himself staring into the "abyss of absolute void" and of the "horrible devil-like being"[37] he encountered. In some of the other accounts it is noteworthy that there are patients who claim to possess the same kind of psychic talents as Dr. Motoyama—telepathic abilities and the capacity to communicate with the spirit world. There is also a significant correspondence between the statement by the woman who reported that doctors had removed her astral body and Dr. Motoyama's statement that his astral body was able to leave his body after he had awakened the Sahasrara chakra.

Meaningful correlations can also be found between my experiences and some who have been in the grips of madness. In her autobiography, *I Never Promised You a Rose Garden*, Joanne Greenberg (Hannah Green), powerfully portrays the internal workings of a mind that has lost its moorings. She brings her principal character, Debra Blau, into confrontation with some of the devastating forces of the mind from the very beginning of her book, on page 4:

> . . . a voice shrieked out of the deep Pit: *Innocent! Innocent!* From freedom, Deborah Blau smashed headlong into the collision of the two worlds. As always before it was a weirdly silent shattering. In the world where she was most alive, the sun split in the sky, the earth erupted, her body was torn to pieces, her teeth and bones crazed and broken to fragments.[38]

This sounds as if I could have written it. Here is my account once again:

> The power of the storms had increased, and the sky inside me had gone totally wild. All became dark, the heavens crackled; I felt my teeth shattering, then there was one deafening thunderclap and like a glass figure inside which the pressure had become too great, I exploded, shattering into a thousand shards of glass. . . .[39]

The psychiatric texts are replete with cases of disintegration. John Frosch, M.D., who has been associated with the

Bellevue Hospital Medical Center and the Department of Psychiatry at the New York University School of Medicine, and who is the author of a book titled *The Psychotic Process*, further demonstrates that these kinds of shattering are not isolated incidents. Here are two of his patients as described in a section called "Fear of Disintegration and Fragmentation": "One of my patients had severe body-image distortions with an omnipresent feeling of not being together. The threat of any illness threw him into panic lest he become fragmented and fall apart."[40] In the second account, interestingly, the patient perceives the disintegration, but is able to prevent it.

> A borderline patient was sitting on a couch opposite a person who was saying things that enraged her. I thought at first she was holding onto the couch to control her destructive impulses against h᷄ · adversary. Actually, it turned out that this was tu prevent herself from falling apart if she let go the couch. With her mounting rage, she suddenly felt as if her body were a mosaic made up of thousands of little pieces which would spring apart if she let go the couch.[41]

When I came out of the shattering, I found myself in an unbelievable state. "My head was off, lying above my right shoulder; my legs were severed from the trunk and lay to the side of where they should be; my left arm was off too. . . ."[42] Deborah Blau too, experienced this kind of bodily distortion. "She lost track of the parts of her body; where her arms were and how to move them."[43] Another patient in our survey said "her arms and legs had been taken off and replaced by artificial flesh."[44] Another woman, the same patient previously described who felt that her body was being punctured, "saw a black devil and had the feeling that her head was being separated from her torso."[45] Serko, in his mescaline experimentation, described a similar experience. He felt that his foot had suddenly become separated from his leg; he could sense it lying below the leg from which it had been severed. Then, he sensed that his head was swivelling around. The next moment, his head had swivelled right off and was free and clear, floating in the air.[46]

Other patient experiences corresponded to the ominous hum I heard, to the rippling floor beneath my feet, to the hundreds of whispering voices in the wall, and to the fire that burned me to the core. The patient already described, who felt an electric kind of heat in her head when the radio was playing also reported a "sound in her ear, and [that] her spine was not in order."[47] A patient "complained that the floorboards were so wavey that there must be water underneath."[48] A woman stated that she had to defend "herself against thousands of voices shouting at her saying there are no sins in her family."[49] Another woman felt "she was being burned alive when she was in packs."[50]

In the foregoing accounts, I tried to avoid depictions of specifically delusional behavior for the most part, in order to focus only on those symptoms *shared* by kundalini and madness. But in fact, the shadow of delusion accompanied many of the patient accounts, and I discovered that delusional and nondelusional thinking are not always as clearly circumscribed as I had expected they would be. For instance, in the preceding paragraph, one of the patients claimed that the floors were so wavy that there must be water underneath. The wavy floors, of course, match my narrative of rippling floors, but are they in themselves indicative of delusional thinking? For instance, I knew that the floors were wavy only in the context of my altered state; I did not take them to "be" wavy, rather, I was perceiving an aspect of the floors previously unknown to me. Such altered perceptions are fairly common in the annals of psychiatry, mysticism, and altered states of consciousness, and my contention is that they should not necessarily be considered delusional. Some psychiatrists understand this distinction, as will be illustrated in the reality-testing model from Dr. Frosch's book, *The Psychotic Process*. But the tendency among psychiatrists seems to be to consider these kinds of states as delusional. This viewpoint notwithstanding, one can postulate other reasons for perceiving that the floor is wavy besides madness, such as that the perceiver could have tuned into a higher vibrational frequency.

In truth, however, little is known about such occurrences. What can be factually stated in my case, is that the perceptions, even though altered, were reality-oriented. I believe, therefore, that my perceptions must be taken at face value and should not be considered delusional. If, however, I were to insist that the floors actually were rippling in the context of physical reality as it is ordinarily perceived, this would have to be diagnosed as delusional thinking. The notion that the floors actually were wavy and that this was caused by water underneath the floor would not be reality based and, therefore, must also be considered delusional. Delusion, in fact, was a frequent component in the patient descriptions, and kept finding its way into the accounts I was focusing on in spite of my efforts to seek only nondelusional patient narratives. Nevertheless, delusion is not always present in altered states of consciousness, and in those instances where delusion is absent, it seems questionable that madness is truly present. For eventually one realizes that it is precisely this delusional thinking that places the mark of madness upon the mind. It is important, therefore, to consider this issue not just in order to comprehend the delusional process, but also with respect to asking about our two groups: Why did the patient group tend to lose sight of reality while in the kundalini narratives, this was never an issue, and in the absence of delusions, can some of the similarities we have witnessed, for instance, the sensation of internal burning, be considered as common denominators uniting the two groups? In order to answer these questions, let us first look at some other examples of specifically delusional thinking.

A woman "explained that she was unjustifiably being accused, for, although she had once received too much change in a store, she had gone right back and reported the error."[51] Despite this people now accuse her of shoplifting and everyone now looks at her strangely. False stories have been printed about her in the newspaper, even though she hasn't killed anyone.

"A man wanted to jump out of a train" and entered a clinic. "He was afraid of being beaten . . . and also admitted to hearing voices."[52] He subsequently attempted suicide several times, proclaimed that he was not a communist, heard plans being made to murder him, and asked to be killed rather than to be slowly tortured.

A woman announced that she was the Empress and would "give birth to King Ludwig and the Prince Regent. . . . every night her stomach was cut open and her breasts cut off; the doctor was really . . . [a preacher] who had beat her and made her pregnant. She also heard voices, saying . . . that she was a murderess. . . . she claimed to have given birth to a tiger with white stripes which was climbing up and down the trees."[53] She presented these ideas in confused, compulsive speech and gave false names to the people around her.

Here is an example from my own experience. One afternoon a man stopped me as I was approaching the building in which I live. He was probably about 35; he clutched a worn briefcase tightly to his body and seemed exhausted, haunted. His suit was frayed around the edges, he was unshaven, and his eyes darted here and there, as if he were on the constant alert. I had the impression of somebody on the run, as if one day he had walked out of his place of employment and never returned. There was an unmistakable aura of desperation about this man. He said, "May I ask you a question?" then lost his courage and started to turn away. But I encouraged him to go ahead. He then stared deeply into my eyes, trying to penetrate, trying to find his answer there, and then asked his question: "Have you been following me?" After recovering from my initial shock I assured the man that I had never seen him in my life. Of course, nothing could have reassured this man, for he was delusional. Typically, he probably could be described as suffering from paranoid delusions, which is a common diagnosis for people who believe they are being followed, watched, or persecuted in some way.

It is difficult to say why one person may become delusional and confused over issues that are not even problematic for another person. A piece of cake is placed in front of two people. One person enjoys the cake and the other person decides that the cake has been poisoned. One person perceives kundalini as a healing, bioelectric current of energy passing through the body and another person feels that someone is trying to electrocute him or her. It may be that a delusional person is more self-centered, less able to see the broader perspective; it may be a problem of self integration.

Gopi Krishna suggests that delusions may be the result of a morbid kundalini awakening due to "overindulgence or an unhealthy state of the reproductive organs."[54] When this happens, the flowing kundalini becomes toxic. Gopi Krishna writes, "With the flow of polluted pranic radiation into the brain, the lights become blinding glares, the sounds distracting noises and shrieks, the visions nightmares, deep insights become crazy whims. The glimpses of a new existence . . . and spiritual exaltation assume the form of grandiose delusions of rank and power."[55]

Joseph Campbell, in his book *Myths to Live By*, offers another reason for delusions.[56] In a chapter titled "Schizophrenia—The Inward Journey" he cites a paper by Dr. Julian Silverman of the National Institute of Mental Health, about an "essential schizophrenia" and a "paranoid schizophrenia," which is to say, a "nondelusional" and a "delusional" schizophrenia. In the paper, appearing in the *American Anthropologist*, Dr. Silverman writes, "In the [essential schizophrenia] state, the profoundest of emotional upheavals and often abounding religious and magical ideation unfold under conditions of marked environmental detachment . . ."[57] Because the *essential schizophrenic* is turned inward, there is a greater likelihood of working through and dealing with the symptoms. But, in "the paranoid schizophrenic type, the psychotic adjustment is quite different. . . . The paranoid schizophrenic, unable to comprehend or tolerate the stark terror of his inner world,"[58] turns outward and finds cause for the chaos occurring internally in outside forces or persons. This is quite like our very first patient, who, because she was burning, ascribed someone who "pushed" her into the flames. In other words, according to Dr. Silverman, the patient creates a delusional setting in the outside world to account for the internal chaos. Thus, Dr. Silverman clearly delineates a delusional and a nondelusional mode of schizophrenia.

Whatever the answer with regard to the cause of delusions, it is manifestly obvious that in the matter of kundalini it is vitally important to see clearly, to have a strong sense of self, and to have an unremitting desire to know what is real, to see the true as true, and the false as false. For at the crossroads separating madness from higher states of consciousness, it seems apparent that the signpost pointing downward reads *Delusions*.

Since Gopi Krishna, Krishnamurti, Dr. Motoyama, and I were not delusional, it seems clear that we were not mad. We had merely activated kundalini. And the symptoms of kundalini can be every bit as dramatic and overwhelming as those of madness. Many symptoms of kundalini, in fact, as we have seen, are indistinguishable from madness. Actually, after comparing the two groups, the term *kundalini* seems to be as valid a term as *psychosis* with respect to our patients, certainly, at least, with regard to any and all patients who were not delusional, and probably even with regard to those patients who were delusional.

Dr. Lee Sannella, a psychiatrist and ophthalmologist, indirectly brings up this same issue, whether kundalini can be compared to psychosis, in a book titled *Kundalini—Psychosis or Transcendence?*[59] The primary focus of this book is on kundalini as transcendence, however, and an investigation of psychosis per se is not undertaken. The book is relevant to our discussion, nevertheless, for it does point to the same question we have been driving at, namely, whether kundalini and psychosis are one and the same thing, and it goes indicate recognition of this issue by a certain sector of the psychiatric community. Unfortunately, the author does not delineate an unequivocal answer to the question the title of his book raises. I believe, however, that the presentation in this chapter strongly suggests that the answer to Dr. Sannella's question is that kundalini is *both* transcendence *and* psychosis. From a symptomatic standpoint, much of the preceding evidence supports this view. The outcomes described in the patient and kundalini accounts differed, true, but that was due to a multitude of factors unrelated to kundalini, not the least of which was delusion. The operative ingredient in every case, even where the patient was decidedly delusional, could still be called kundalini. Some of the other factors, such as individual backgrounds, personal circumstances, dietary habits, physical makeup, education, intellectual capacity, basic nature, spirituality, and so forth, must also be factored into the equation and undoubtedly contributed to whether there was a positive or a negative outcome. Whatever particulars are brought to bear, though, it seems plain that the patient who felt pulled by the hair at the back of her neck and at the same time saw a great flame flare up from the depths was riding the same roller coaster as Gopi Krishna when he closed his eyes to see a large tongue of flame leap across his spine into his head. Whether the end result was disorientation or illumination, the precipitating agent in each instance was kundalini. Kundalini *can* be equated with psychosis. And if the precipitating agent is kundalini, then the diagnosis of psychosis is erroneous. So we are now faced with the issue of the impact that such a diagnosis may have upon individuals whose symptoms in reality indicate an aroused kundalini.

Clearly, psychosis is not an acceptable definition for the manifestations of kundalini. Not only does it stigmatize the person in whom the kundalini is becoming active, which is to say that it denigrates what is essentially a spiritual process, but it leads to institutionalization and deliberate attempts to suppress what is also a healing process, the awakening kundalini. This is not to say that professional assistance is unnecessary. People who have been caught in the powerful maelstrom of kundalini do need help, especially in those cases where there has been excessive difficulty, or where there has been a morbid or delusional arousal. But the right kind of help is required. Assistance should take place in a non-institutional environment, should be spiritually oriented, should be handled by physicians knowledgeable about kundalini and who are skilled at guiding patients through the process, not stifling it with the methodology of psychiatry.

Joseph Campbell in *Myths to Live by*, in the chapter on schizophrenia previously cited, focuses on a paper by John Weir Perry, M.D., of the University of California Medical School in San Francisco, in support of this view. The paper appeared in the *Annals of the New York Academy of Sciences* and came to Campbell's attention as the result of a dual talk he and Perry gave at the Esalen Institute in Big Sur, California. Campbell writes:

> Now it was Dr. Perry's thesis in his paper that in certain cases the best thing is to let the schizo-phrenic process run its course, not to abort the psychosis by administering shock treatments and the like, but, on the contrary, to help the process of disintegration and reintegration along. However, if a doctor is to be helpful in this way, he has to understand the image language of mythology. He has himself to understand what the fragmentary signs and signals signify that his patient, totally out of touch with rationally oriented manners of thought and communication, is trying to bring forth in order to establish some kind of contact. Interpreted from this point of view, a schizophrenic break-down is an inward and backward journey to recover something missed or lost, and to restore, thereby, a vital balance. So let the voyager go.

He has tipped over and is sinking, perhaps drowning; yet, as in the old legend of Gilgamesh and his long, deep dive to the bottom of the cosmic sea to pluck the watercress of immortality, there is the one green value of his life down there. Don't cut him off from it: help him through.[60]

Dr. Perry himself writes:

. . . it is, unfortunately, the habit in psychiatric practice to avoid any extensive encounter with the deep psychic contents in the profound disorders of the psychoses. . . .

If we ignore these, the only alternative is to hold the patient up to some external criteria of behavior that we impose upon him, rather than helping him follow the demands of his own psychic individuality. . . .

My view of my part in therapeutic outcome is that I should help nature in its own strange and unfamiliar devices to effect a reestablishment of the self, and thus of the ego. . . . By this, I mean to imply, of course, that there are in the psyche spontaneous processes to reconstitute the self, and that we do best by trying to understand these and facilitate them.[61]

It is gratifying to find such ideas of what constitutes effective therapy, points of view with which I am in complete accord, presented in the prestigious Annals of the New York Academy of Sciences and in the writings of the eminent mythologist, Joseph Campbell. I realize, though, that the central idea I have been honing here, that psychosis is actually a manifestation of kundalini, remains yet to be proven. So far I have shown the striking similarities between kundalini and the symptoms of so-called madness, which in itself does not prove them to be one and the same thing. The term for madness, for psychosis, most in use today, is the word *schizophrenia*, meaning "splitting of the mind," which has replaced the nineteenth century term *dementia praecox* (premature dementia). In chapter 7, then, I will turn to the schizophrenia that is the focus of Silverman's, Campbell's, and Perry's interest. There I will trace the similarities between kundalini and schizophrenia to their root, to the very heart and core of madness. There, out among the smoking bonfires of the disintegrated psyche, I believe that I shall be able to prove my thesis, that kundalini and madness, or schizophrenia, are essentially the same thing. Admittedly, this is a startling idea. But the implications, in terms of health for the mentally afflicted, are equally startling.

Over the past few pages we have witnessed some dramatic testimony from people who inadvertently sailed out beyond the dropping off point. Most of them would not have ventured into those waters voluntarily. One cannot help but admire the courage that these seafarers summoned at a moment's notice to deal with their situations. It seems clear that every single one of these good citizens found themselves in the selfsame waters. Why is it that some became disoriented, in danger of drowning, while others were able to swim? Why is it that some found only darkness and madness in those waters, while others found inspiration and transformation?

One answer has been supplied by Dr. John Frosch, whose model for defining psychosis is helpful in zeroing in on the demarcation line separating malignant from wholesome or potentially wholesome mental states. "It should be clear by now that I believe that the presence of psychosis to a large extent hinges on the loss of the capacity to test reality. . . . Obviously the nature of the danger and the modes of dealing with this danger are important in psychosis, but to my mind, reality testing is the ultimate criterion. Its loss is psychosis. Its presence doesn't mean that psychopathology, even severe psychopathology doesn't exist. But the person who retains a consistent capacity to test reality is not psychotic." Dr. Frosch extends this standard even to so-called hallucinations. "It is conceivable that a hallucination . . . may not be accompanied by a loss in the capacity to test reality."[62]

I like Dr. Frosch's test even though obviously I cannot agree with the concept to which he adheres—psychosis. But his test is applicable, for instance, when considering why Gopi Krishna was able to bring his kundalini to a successful conclusion, while the patient who accused someone of pushing her into the flames ended up lost and deluded in a mental institution.

In concluding this chapter, the salient feature of the kundalini-madness, or kundalini-schizophrenia, syndrome I would most like to point to is that kundalini is healing when given the opportunity to run its full course. For as the four kundalini narratives have confirmed, the fires of kundalini may seem at first to be the fires of madness, but later as the night cools, a golden flame begins to light the sky, burning off the residues of ignorance that blind the human spirit.

• • • • •

Before continuing with this issue of whether or not psychosis is symptomatic of kundalini awakening, it will be necessary to pause a moment to discuss kundalini in an historical context. This we will do in chapter 6. During this brief interlude, we will follow the serpent path through the early civilizations of the world. This little side trip is of consequence to the discussion to follow in chapter 7, for at this juncture I believe it is important to build evidential support for the kundalini phenomenon, to provide a more substantial, scientifically accredited base from which kundalini may seriously contend against the belief systems of professional psychiatry. For we shall discover certain unproven, yet very definite beliefs, certain sacred principles of orthodox psychiatry, standing solidly in opposition to our contention that kundalini and schizophrenia are one and the same thing.

Our guides on this journey through the ancient past will be the renowned scholar, writer, and teacher of mythology, Joseph Campbell, and author, editor, and scholar, Gene Kieffer, who has written numerous essays and treatises about the ancient myths as they apply to kundalini.

Chapter 6

Dextra Dei:
The Kundalini of Joseph Campbell

Kundalini has been known as a spiritual phenomenon for thousands of years. This has been well documented by Joseph Campbell, conceivably the world's foremost authority on mythology at the time of his death on October 31, 1987. Gene Kieffer, in his treatise *The Evolution of Joseph Campbell and America*, points out that Campbell had become fascinated by the kundalini motif during the latter part of his life. Thereafter, Campbell featured kundalini in two of his books, *The Mythic Image* and *The Inner Reaches of Outer Space*, and frequently mentioned kundalini. Campbell stated that "kundalini can be found in almost all cultures on every continent, dating from even before the dawn of civilization."[1] In *The Mythic Image*, Campbell writes:

> . . . the earliest known evidences of yoga appear on a half-dozen or so of the Indus Valley seals (2500–1500 B.C.), an example of which appears here. [See figure 3 on page 108.] Two attendant serpents elevate their giant forms behind a pair of worshipers kneeling at either hand of an enthroned figure seated in what appears to be a posture of yoga. And the fact that the elevation of the so-called Serpent Power is one of the

Figure 3. An Indus Valley Seal, known as *Deity with Worshipers and Serpents*, ca. 2000 B.C. Reproduced from *The Mythic Image* by Joseph Campbell, Bollingen Series C (Princeton, NJ: Princeton University Press, 1974).

Figure 4. Drawing after a Sumerian Ritual Cup depicting the Mesopotamian serpent-god, Ningishzida, entwined about an axial rod. Reproduced from *The Mythic Image* by Joseph Campbell, Bollingen Series C (Princeton, NJ: Princeton University Press, 1974).

leading motifs of yogic symbolism suggests that we may have here an explicit pictorial reference not only to the legend of some prehistoric yogi, but also to the unfoldment through yoga of this subtle spiritual force.

If so, the question arises whether some sort of yoga may not have been practiced outside India at that time as well. For a number of the symbols that are interpreted in psychological terms in yogic lore appear also in the monuments of other ancient cultures . . .

Here, for example is an ornamented Sumerian ritual cup of the same period as the Indus Valley seal. [See figure 4.] Two composite beasts . . . draw back the portals of a sanctuary, where an apparition appears of the great Mesopotamian serpent-god Ningishzida. . . . The two are entwined about an axial rod in such a way as to suggest both the caduceus of classical Hermes, guide of souls to rebirth in eternal life, and the Indian diagram of seven spinal centers touched and awakened to consciousness in Kundalini yoga by the rising Serpent Power.[2]

The spinal centers are, of course, integral to the kundalini process as it has been depicted down through the ages and would be a central point of focus for any serious inquiry into the kundalini mystique. Joseph Campbell was well aware of the relevance of these centers "and demonstrated time and time again that he knew that the deepest levels of the cerebro-spinal system are involved in the process of spiritual transformation."[3] This can be seen not only in his general analysis of the kundalini system, but also in his citation of Sri Ramakrishna to illustrate the process of kundalini arousal.

Campbell referred to Ramakrishna, who was one of the great Indian sages of the nineteenth century, as "a veritable virtuoso"[4] in the practice of kundalini Yoga. By the example of his own life, Ramakrishna documented on a daily basis that the kundalini energy actually does rise through the spinal centers. Kieffer illustrates this by quoting from Campbell's *The Inner Reaches of Outer Space*:

> . . . at some point the body and mind together become fundamentally aware and convinced that *the energy by which the body is pervaded is the same as that which illuminates the world and maintains alive all beings.* . . . Ramakrishna has described the actual sensation . . . :[5]
> "Sometimes the Spiritual Current rises through the spine, crawling like an ant. Sometimes, in Samādhi, the soul swims joyfully in the ocean of divine ecstasy, like a fish. Sometimes, when I lie down on my side, I feel the Spiritual Current pushing me like a monkey and playing with me joyfully. I remain still. That current, like a monkey, suddenly with one jump reaches the Sahasrāra. That is why you see me jump up with a start. Sometimes, again, the Spiritual Current rises like a bird hopping from one branch to another. The place where it rests feels like fire. . . . Sometimes the Spiritual Current moves up like a snake. Going in a zigzag way, at last it reaches the head and I go into Samadhi. A man's spiritual consciousness is not awakened unless his Kundalinī is aroused."[6]

In regard to the spinal centers, Ramakrishna wrote, "it had been revealed to me how the Kundalini is aroused, how the lotuses of the different centers blossom forth, and how all this culminates in samadhi."[7]

Campbell follows Ramakrishna's words with his own extremely enthusiastic analysis of the process by which the kundalini rises from the Muladhara to the Sahasrara. He writes:

> . . . *kundalinī* is *essential spiritual energy* pictured as a coiled white serpent asleep in the *mūlādhāra* of each of us. Serpents shed their skins, as the moon its shadow, to be as it were reborn. . . . The continuous flashing of their fiery forked tongues testifies to the trapped light within them. Hence, the uncoiling "Serpent Power," *kundalinī*, ascending the *sushumnā* to unite at the crown of our head with the lotus "Thousand Petaled," *sahasrāra*, "bright with the brightness of ten million suns," is equivalent . . . to the moon approaching its fifteenth night, when its light will match that of the sun. *Kundalinī* and *Sahasrāra* therewith unite as one. . . ."[8]

Campbell then goes on to describe kundalini as a "highly sophisticated and effective, spiritually transformative degree."[9] Author Kieffer infers that over time, kundalini came to be everything for Campbell. The following quotation, which Kieffer also culls from *The Inner Reaches of Outer Space*, supports the kundalini point of view with equal enthusiasm, but from a historical perspective this time.

> And so, indeed, it does appear that anyone viewing with unprejudiced eye the religions of mankind must recognize mythic themes at every hand that are shared, though differently

interpreted, among the peoples of this planet.
... C. G. Jung, as we have also remarked, proposed his theory of "archetypes of the unconscious" [to explain such correspondences].

[But] there are, however, instances that cannot be so readily interpreted in purely psychological terms, as for example in the matter of our present interest, [kundalini] where a structured constellation of ideas, images, and related exercises, yielding transformational experiences will have appeared over an extensive historical field ... unmistakably of one originating structure.

For it is evident that knowledge of what is known today in India as the *kundalinī* was not in ancient times confined to the Indus Valley Civilization.[10]

Kieffer traces this extensive historical field—kundalini—beyond the Indus Valley and still further in *The Inner Reaches of Outer Space*. For in this volume Campbell also catalogued "a large number of examples where the Serpent Power was paramount in various civilizations, from India to nearby Mesopotamia, then Egypt and Ireland and throughout the four quarters of the globe."[11] Campbell writes:

There is in the Musée Guimet, in Paris, from China of the Chou Dynasty, c. 1027–256 BC, a coiled bronze serpent ... showing just three and one-half turns, which to me at least, very strongly suggests the *kundalinī* in the *mūlā-dhāra*. And at the opposite margin of the vast Eurasian common-culture field, in Ireland, ninth century AD, not only were the enigmatic illuminations of the Book of Kells made alive

with symbolic serpents . . . but also, on the side
of an immense stone cross of the same pre-
Gothic Christian period—the "Cross of [the
abbot] Muiredach," . . . there was engraved in
high relief an astonishing panel . . . known as
Dextra Dei, the "Right Hand of God," in which
two interlacing serpents appear, one heading
downward, the other upward, enframing three
human heads in ascending series, with a
human right hand above, reaching to the center of a crowning, halolike, ornamented disk. If
this is not an explicit reference to the top four
states of an ascent of the *sushumnā*, the sense of
such an appearance on a Christian monument
commemorating the Crucifixion remains to be
explained.[12] (See figure 5 on page 114.)

Kieffer delves further, inquiring whether kundalini was
known to the Navajos and Maya. "[Campbell] didn't
offer a definitive answer. Kundalini yoga was practiced
in the Early Bronze Age of the Near and Middle East, certainly, but knowledge of it may have existed even earlier
and at other places. Campbell found strong evidence for
it in South America, among the Maya and the Aztec people, and in North America as well.[13] For example, he
wrote, [There is] "the Navaho sand painting . . . where
the imagery and connotations so perfectly match those of
the ascent of the *sushumnā* that if the painting had come
from Tibet, instead of from New Mexico, an immediate
connection [to kundalini] could be assumed without
hesitation."[14] (See figure 6 on page 115.)

Joseph Campbell has portrayed kundalini as real
and undeniable. For we have seen in his writings that
there are cultural and historical precedents for affirming
the existence of kundalini as a religious reality in various

Figure 5. Dextra Dei, "The Right Hand of God," an engraving on the immense stone Cross of the Abbot Muriedach and Cross of the Monasterboice Louth, A.D. tenth century. From *Irish Art during the Viking Invasions* (*800-1020 A.D.*) by Françoise Henry (Ithaca, NY: Cornell University Press,

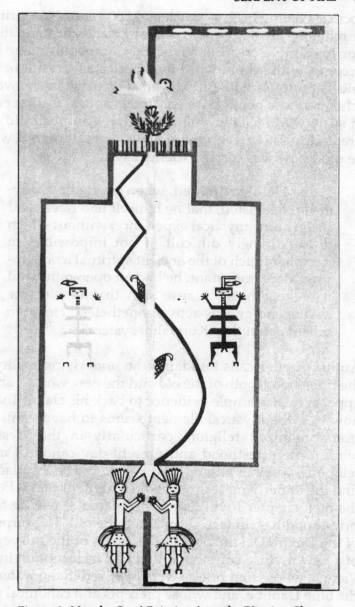

Figure 6. Navaho Sand Painting from the Blessing Chant, c. 1950. Reproduced from *The Pollen Path* by Margaret Schevill Link (Stanford, CA: Stanford University Press, 1956).

societies dating back as much as 4,500 years. No spiritual or religious ideology could ask for greater substantiation, nor for a more credible advocate. Campbell's name has become a household word in America as a result of the television series with Bill Moyers. Furthermore, he was a scholar whose books have enormous appeal in all sectors of society. Mr. Kieffer points out that Campbell did not pretend to know everything about kundalini, but what he did know was certain. Kieffer says:

> . . . he plainly admitted, when queried by Moyers on television, that he himself had never had the genuine mystical experience, without which it is extremely difficult, if not impossible, to decipher much of the ancient spiritual iconography. More important, he had an open mind and a seeking heart, a sure sign that in him the divine energy was active nonetheless. He often talked about the "Kundalini system". . . .[15]

Author Kieffer calls kundalini the underlying reality of the priesthood, both of the old and the new worlds, and it appears he has ample evidence to back his claim. Today, however, the mystical element seems to have vanished from organized religion, particularly in the Western world. The priesthood and present-day canon of most religions, whether East or West, would not be the place to find the underlying reality of which Kieffer speaks. For in the next chapter I will demonstrate that a new de facto priesthood has, in fact, supplanted the old. The serpents of the Dextra Dei are now in the hands of the purveyors of a new myth, a priesthood that had its inception in old Vienna, whose first priests were baptized in the waters of the blue Danube, and whose precepts and canonical procedures were first delineated in the collected works of

Sigmund Freud. Thus, a new cosmology has arisen, presided over by Super Ego, Ego, and Id, peopled by the free-floating thought forms of repressed emotional trauma, monitored in the lower realms by Oedipus Rex and in the higher realms by Jungian archetypes of the unconscious. This is the matrix from which present-day psychiatric practice has evolved. Search as one may, however, in the psychocosmology of today's clinicians, the serpents of the Dextra Dei are nowhere to be found. For every attempt has been made to expunge them, from frontal lobotomies to electroshock therapy to antipsychotic drugs. In the next chapter we shall try to discover these serpents of fire in their twentieth century lairs and see if we can discern in their lithesome uncoiling the transformational processes that so beguiled Joseph Campbell.

Chapter 7

Serpent in the Snake Pit:
Kundalini Vis-à-Vis Schizophrenia

Evidence of kundalini as it commonly manifests today, may be more readily located in the case files of psychotherapists, psychoanalysts, and psychiatrists than anywhere else. For as illustrated in chapters 3 and 5, mystical states are often accompanied by a great deal of turmoil; and the usual and accepted places for seeking relief from this kind of turmoil are the offices of these physicians. If the turmoil becomes extreme, it can result in a diagnosis of manic-depressive psychosis or schizophrenia, and the individual so diagnosed may wind up on the ward of a mental hospital. Mental hospitals are, of course, governed by psychiatrists, who have the power to make clinical diagnoses and to determine treatment procedures. It could be argued, then, that psychiatry is literally the priesthood of today, for these are the practitioners who are entrusted with caring for some of the most spiritually advanced members of society. This is not to state that a diagnosis of mental illness in itself indicates spirituality. Nevertheless, many patients in the care of mental health professionals do seem to possess a strong affinity for the paranormal and are unusually gifted at finding their way to transcendental states of mind.

We have already seen that the symptoms of kundalini and madness (schizophrenia) are strikingly similar. They are so similar that one could easily infer that schizophrenia is, in fact, nothing less than a specific phase in the kundalini process. Given that individuals in whom kundalini has become active may, therefore, find themselves diagnosed as schizophrenic and in the hands of psychiatrists, it is imperative that we take a close look at psychiatric attitudes toward such states of mind.

The work of E. Fuller Torrey is representative of this general approach. He is a traditional, clinical psychiatrist. His views on the cause and treatment of schizophrenia—in short, that schizophrenia is a disease of the brain best treated with various drug therapies—probably resonates pretty well with the general viewpoint of psychiatry. Dr. Torrey has a long list of credits, including four years of service as a Special Assistant to the Director of the National Institute of Mental Health, eight years as a clinical psychiatrist at St. Elizabeths Hospital in Washington, DC, nomination of one of his books to the National Book Critics Circle, and appearances on national television.

Very broadly, Torrey's approach consists of first diagnosing if the patient's symptoms indicate actual psychosis, and if so, then determining what kind of psychosis it is. Traditionally, organized psychiatry divides psychoses into manic-depressive psychosis and schizophrenia, although many psychiatrists suspect that the two psychoses are each just opposite ends of one continuum, which is to say that in reality, only one psychosis—madness—exists. In this text we will only focus on schizophrenia, proceeding from this view that only one psychosis exists. In other words, we will regard schizophrenia and manic-depressive psychosis as part of one indivisible process. By focusing on schizophrenia we will also be covering those areas, such as manic or depressive behavior, that are called manic-depressive psychosis.

Torrey's procedure, if the diagnosis is schizophrenia, may include drug therapy, hospitalization, if it is thought necessary, and out-patient psychiatric services. Torrey does not believe that psychoanalysis or insight-oriented psychotherapy is effective in the treatment of schizophrenia.

Let us go to Torrey's first step, and see how he goes about deciding whether a person has schizophrenia. In his book, *Surviving Schizophrenia, A Family Manual*, Torrey lists the following seven symptoms which are typically described by individuals with schizophrenia.

1) Alterations of the senses

2) Inability to sort and interpret incoming sensations, and an inability therefore to respond appropriately

3) Delusions and hallucinations

4) Altered sense of self

5) Changes in emotions

6) Changes in movements

7) Changes in behavior[1]

Torrey states that no single one of these symptoms can be said to exist in all patients with schizophrenia; some patients show more of one symptom, other patients exhibit another. He also states that these symptoms can also be found occasionally in patients with certain other diseases of the brain, such as brain tumors and temporal lobe epilepsy.

Let us now see if Torrey's list of symptoms supports what I wish to infer, that schizophrenia is a certain phase of kundalini. What follows is a comparison of the symptoms presented by schizophrenic patients to the symptoms described in the kundalini narratives in order to see whether both groups share a common cause.

This first account is from *Diary of a Schizophrenic Girl*, by Margaret Sechehaye and is used by Torrey to illustrate symptom 7, changes in behavior. Sechehaye's report is reminiscent of my description of the tapestry, from which I fled, perceiving that it was dark and foreboding, that the weave had begun to crawl and undulate, and that the apartment had become a living, breathing entity. Here is Dr. Sechehaye's patient, Renée:

> As a matter of fact, these "things" weren't doing anything special; they didn't speak, nor attack me directly. It was their very presence that made me complain. I saw things, smooth as metal, so cut off, so detached from each other, so illuminated and tense that they filled me with terror. When, for example, I looked at a chair or a jug . . . they became "things" and began to take on life, to exist . . . people asked specifically, "Do you see the jug and the chair as alive?" I answered, "Yes, they are alive." And they, the doctors too, thought I saw these things as humans whom I heard speak. But it was not that. Their life consisted uniquely in the fact that they were there, in their existence itself. To flee from them I hid my head in my hands or stood in a corner.[2]

In listing the following examples Torrey is focusing on symptom 1, Alterations of the senses. In the first account (a) this manifests as "heightened awareness," which Torrey says many patients describe during the initial days after the onset of schizophrenia. In the second account (b) problems in concentration are described, resulting from the senses becoming overly acute. The first description (a) sounds like Gopi Krishna's sense of being immersed in a sea of light; the second description (b) is quite like Gopi Krishna's difficulties in focusing his thoughts following the initial activation of his kundalini. Here are Torrey's accounts:

(a) Suddenly my whole being was filled with light and loveliness and with an upsurge of deeply moving feeling from within myself to meet and reciprocate the influence that flowed into me. I was in a state of the most vivid awareness and illumination. What can I say of it? A cloudless, cerulean blue sky of the mind, shot through with shafts of exquisite, warm, dazzling sunlight.[3]

(b) My concentration is very poor. I jump from one thing to another. If I am talking to someone they only need to cross their legs or scratch their heads and I am distracted and forget what I was saying. I think I could concentrate better with my eyes shut.[4]

In the next account, Torrey's interest is symptom 4, Altered sense of self, which he says is characteristic of many schizophrenic patients. This description is similar to Krishnamurti's revelation where he became the man working on the road, the very pickaxe the workman held in his hand, and the little ant crawling on a blade of grass. Here is the patient:

I saw myself in different bodies. . . . The night nurse came in and sat under the shaded lamp in the quiet ward. I recognized her as me, and I watched for some time quite fascinated; I had never had an outside view of myself before. In the morning several of the patients having breakfast were me. I recognized them by the way they held their knives and forks.[5]

In the following case, Torrey illustrates symptom 3, Delusions and hallucinations. Intimations of Dr. Motoyama's chakras, too, can be seen in this patient's description.

At an early stage the appearance of colored flashes of light was common. These took the form either of distant streaks or of nearby round glowing patches about a foot in diameter.[6]

Torrey also presents numerous examples of auditory hallucinations from various case histories. These were experienced by Gopi Krishna, Krishnamurti, and Dr. Motoyama in the form of autonomous sounds and voices coming from within, and by me as voices coming from outside myself.

The same concordance exists between Torrey's case studies and the four kundalini narratives that was in evidence in the previous patient descriptions in chapter 5. Not only do the patient and kundalini accounts agree on a one-to-one basis, but the kundalini descriptions fit into Torrey's classifications of symptoms typically described by patients with schizophrenia. Thus my symptoms can be listed under symptom 7, Changes in behavior, Gopi Krishna's symptoms can be listed under symptom 1, Alterations of the senses, Krishnamurti's symptoms can be listed under symptom 4, Altered sense of self, and Dr. Motoyama's symptoms can be listed under symptom 3, Delusions and hallucinations. Thus, our prototypes' experiences fit four categories of symptoms in Torrey's schizophrenia model.

Let us now see if the symptoms described in the kundalini narratives will fit into Torrey's remaining three categories: (2) Inability to sort and interpret incoming sensations, and an inability therefore to respond appropriately; (5) Changes in emotions; and (6) Changes in movements. Under symptom 2, I found no correspondences. Under symptom 5, however, which Torrey calls "one of the most common and characteristic changes in schizophrenia . . . . especially prominent in the later stages of the disease" and during which the "patient may feel widely varying and rapidly fluctuating emotions" accompanied frequently by "pervasive and nameless fear,"[7] I submit the following quote from Gopi Krishna: "My consciousness was in such a state of unceasing flux that I was never certain how it would behave within the next few minutes. It rose and fell like a wave, raising me one moment out of the clutches of fear to dash me again the next into the depths of despair."[8] Torrey also lists flattening or blunting of emotion in this category. Gopi Krishna says, "I lost all feeling of love for my wife and children. I had loved them fondly from the depths of my being. The fountain of love in me seemed to have dried up completely."[9]

Under symptom 6, Torrey lists catatonic behavior as one of the most dramatic symptoms. Dr. Motoyama has described catatonic-type states. In one such instance, while playing a Japanese game called *Kokkurisan* (similar to Ouija Board), he "fell into a semi-trance. [His] body felt like it was on fire and [he] began to sweat profusely."[10] Soon his right arm began to shake uncontrollably, the trance deepened, and then he had a vision which lasted another ten to twenty minutes—the trance state lasted throughout.

These correspondences must be considered meaningful. As a group, Gopi Krishna, Krishnamurti, Dr. Motoyama, and I have demonstrated six of the seven symptoms that Torrey has listed as being characteristic of the symptoms of schizophrenia. In other words, the symptoms narrated by us cover pretty much the entire range of schizophrenic behavior. Individually, we each present three, four, or more of these symptoms. Krishnamurti, for instance, experienced first, Alteration of the senses, that is, heightened awareness and "God intoxication," leading to what Torrey calls "religious preoccupation"; second, Delusions and hallucinations, in which other entities carried on conversations in his head; third, Altered sense of self, where he was out of his body seeing himself in other people's bodies; fourth, Changes in emotions, from the distinctly flattened-out emotion of his elemental to the exalted state of his God consciousness; and fifth, Changes in movements, his falling down into dead faints, about which Torrey reports that people who are schizophrenic are much more likely to stumble while walking after the onset of their symptoms.[11] From this analysis, I think it is fairly obvious that we of the kundalini narratives qualify for the diagnosis of schizophrenia. One symptom would be enough in many instances to diagnose an individual as schizophrenic.

Symptomatically then, a case can be made that kundalini and schizophrenia are two sides of a coin. Persons with an aroused kundalini could easily be diagnosed as having schizophrenia. Conversely, many schizophrenic patients could be written into any of the kundalini depictions thus far.

It remains to be seen then, what causes the schizophrenia-kundalini syndrome. We have already observed that the cause of the symptoms of kundalini is the current of kundalini coursing through the brain and body. The cause attributed to schizophrenia, adamantly attributed by Dr. Torrey, is *disease of the brain*.

Torrey comes to the point right away in *Surviving Schizophrenia*. In the second paragraph of his preface to the revised edition, he informs his readers that research has now affirmed more than ever the biological basis for declaring that schizophrenia and manic-depressive psychosis are brain diseases; no more, no less, than are diseases like Parkinson's disease, multiple sclerosis, and Alzheimer's disease.[12]

In the body of the text itself, though, Torrey contradicts this, saying:

> To date we have no single thing which can be measured and from which we can then say: Yes, that is schizophrenia. Because of this, the definition of the disease is a source of great confusion and debate. This confusion is exacerbated because of the likelihood that schizophrenia is more than one disease entity.... Since we do not yet have anything which can be reliably measured to help define schizophrenia, we are left only with its symptoms.[13]

Still later in the text Torrey returns to his "brain disease" theory, asserting that there now exists incontrovertible proof that schizophrenics, as a group, have different kinds of brains than people who are not schizophrenic.[14] Torrey carries his argument further in a section called "Gross Pathology." He notes that observations about abnormalities in the brains of schizophrenics have been intermittently reported since the beginning of the century. Before the present time, however, such observations were the result of examinations carried out at autopsy, as the technology was not available for assessing the brains of live people. Now, however, such technology exists. "Computerized tomography (CT) and nuclear magnetic resonance imaging (MRI) scans" offer nonintrusive, painless capabilities of examining and observing brain structures of people while they are still alive.[15]

In other words, the type and extent of brain disease can now be assessed during a patient's hospitalization. If this were really true in the case of schizophrenia, however, why has Torrey been complaining that schizophrenia can only be defined by its symptoms? Why doesn't he just run to a CT scan, cast a professional eye upon it and say, "Yes, that is schizophrenia"? The answer is that the pathological differences Torrey refers to do not point to a schizophrenia pathology at all; they just point to anatomical variations that have been found in some schizophrenics, such as "enlargement of the lateral ventricles" or "atrophy of a portion of the cerebellum"[16] cited by Torrey in support of his argument. But there is no evidence from which to cite such abnormalities as resulting from, or as a cause for, schizophrenia. Nor does Torrey demonstrate *any* cause for variations like these. He doesn't know what causes them. Further, in order to assert that such abnormalities are schizophrenia, they must be found in all schizophrenics. The spirochete that causes syphilis circulates in the blood of all syphilitics; the pathogen that causes tuberculosis can be found in all individuals with this disease. Torrey does not show any disease symptom common to all schizophrenics. Moreover, when Torrey tries to show such commonality of symptoms, he fails to prove his point. Abnormal EEG readings, impaired gag reflexes, or increased/decreased blinking rates of the eyes, all pointed to by Torrey as common neurological abnormalities in schizophrenia, do not necessarily indicate brain disease or schizophrenia. They may be caused by disease in the brain, and they may occur in some persons with schizophrenia; but then again, they may also occur in persons who do not have schizophrenia. Furthermore, in order to impute brain disease as the cause of these symptoms, and then to call that brain disease schizophrenia, at the very least, evidence of a brain disease must be shown. An effect must have a cause. Torrey is unable to show any cause at all for schizophrenia. He cannot say, "Here, under this microscope is the bacterium, germ, lesion, virus, or whatever, that causes schizophrenia." In other words, Torrey does not know what schizophrenia is beyond its symptomatology. He is calling it a brain disease at his convenience to fit his preconceived notions.

Thus, Torrey's assertions are not convincing; neither are his reports on the various kinds of pathology tests. One such study that Torrey is quick to use to support his cause reaches the conclusion that individuals with schizophrenia have smaller heads, brains, and frontal lobes. But Torrey does not provide data by which the reader may verify such a conclusion. Yet, such assertions must be proved, for certain questions leap instantly to mind, for example, did these individuals have any genetic or brain disorders coincidental to their schizophrenia? What were the criteria for defining this particular group as schizophrenic? Did all of the schizophrenics tested show smaller brains? Torrey, however, does not bring questions like these to his readers' attention, yet he expects the study to be accepted as fact. Further, since smaller brains are generally equated with lesser intelligence, such a conclusion is demeaning to people diagnosed with schizophrenia. In view of Torrey's position on treatment for schizophrenic patients, a stance that includes enforced medication and enforced institutionalization, such a conclusion is not surprising. Consider Torrey's remedy for creating compliance in taking medication. He first details a list of strategies to encourage resistant patients to accept medication. If, however, they remain intractable, Torrey advises that legal steps may be necessary.[17] Given such a viewpoint, it certainly would be to Torrey's advantage if it could be established that schizophrenic individuals actually did have smaller brains than the rest of the population. Legislators would be more amenable to providing the laws Torrey is calling for if the laws concern individuals who have been branded as a kind of subspecies with smaller brains.

Torrey summarizes his presentation of pathology tests by reasserting his litany on brain disease. He writes that "studies of gross pathology, microscopic pathology, neurochemistry, cerebral blood flow, and metabolism, as well as electrical, neurological, and neuropsychological measures"[18] unmistakably demonstrate that schizophrenia is as much a brain disease as Parkinson's disease, Alzheimer's disease, or multiple sclerosis. But Torrey still neglects to provide data by which the reliability of the tests may be judged, nor does he reveal any of the steps of his own analysis of the data from any study or tests. To accept the inferences that Torrey has drawn about these tests and studies requires that one accept his evaluations and reasonings, his thought processes and critical aptitude, and his conclusions on faith. As will be shown next, there may be, in fact, good reason to doubt Torrey's critical judgment in these matters.

Dr. Thomas Szasz, who has been a professor of psychiatry at the State University of New York in Syracuse, is also a practicing psychiatrist and the author of twenty books and hundreds of articles. He is considered one of the foremost writers in present-day psychiatry. In his book *Insanity, The Idea and Its Consequences*, he focuses on the issue of schizophrenia as mental disease. Szasz, who questions whether mental illness names a bona fide illness, says in his preface, "Actually, anyone—even a person quite unfamiliar with psychiatry—could reason that a disease characterized as *mental* must be something other than a bodily disease."[19] He points out that psychiatrists have been maintaining the existence of pathological findings in schizophrenia for more than a century without yet being able to demonstrate the pathological lesions they purport to exist in the brain. Szasz makes the following statements about schizophrenia as a disease:

> Psychiatrists . . . insist that schizophrenia and manic-depressive psychosis are brain diseases. Textbooks of pathology describe and discuss all known bodily diseases, including brain diseases. Accordingly, one way to verify whether schizophrenia and manic-depressive psychosis are brain diseases is to see what the authors of textbooks of pathology say about them. Well, the answer is that they do not say anything at all about these alleged diseases: they do not mention them, as they simply do not recognize mental illnesses as (bodily) diseases. The significance of this much-neglected fact is enhanced by the pathologists' recognition of *mental retardation*— not as a disease, to be sure, but as the manifestation of certain genetic disorders, such as Down's syndrome (formerly known as mongolism). In order to show that the psychiatric claim—now widely shared by lay mental health groups— that the major psychoses are proven brain diseases is completely unsupported by the opinion of pathologists, I have reviewed the principal contemporary textbooks of pathology, with the following result.

Stanley L. Robbins, professor of pathology at Boston University Medical School, is the senior author of what is perhaps the most widely used textbook in the field, *Pathologic Basis of Disease* (3rd ed.). In this work, running to almost 1500 pages, there is no mention of schizophrenia, manic-depression, or any mental illness. Revealingly, the authors, who thus implicitly reject the reality or somatic basis of mental illness, do recognize the reality of the somatic basis of mental retardation: in the chapter on "Genetic Disorders," they describe and discuss Down's syndrome as well as Klinefelter's syndrome (two genetic disorders causing intellectual impairment).

Anderson's Pathology—a two-volume work running to nearly 2000 pages, edited by John M. Kissane, professor of pathology at Washington University in St. Louis—also makes no mention of schizophrenia or manic-depression. Finally, the most comprehensive contemporary text on pathological physiology—*Sodeman's Pathologic Physiology* (7th ed.)—is also completely silent on the subject of schizophrenia and manic-depression. In short, the authors of textbooks on pathological *anatomy*, *biochemistry*, and *physiology* do not mention the major mental illnesses—treating them either as if they did not exist or were not diseases.

Viewed against this background, the claims of clinical psychiatrists—who have no special competence in anatomy, biochemistry, or physiology—may seem less convincing. For example, E. Fuller Torrey, a zealous propagandist for the view that schizophrenia is a brain disease (and for the policy of treating it involuntarily), flatly asserts: "In the last decade research evidence has become overwhelming that these [schizophrenia, manic depressive psychosis] are indeed brain diseases, just as multiple sclerosis, Parkinson's disease, and Alzheimer's disease are brain diseases."

Evidently, Torrey's research evidence has not yet overwhelmed pathologists who write text-books of pathology: as we saw, they recognize multiple sclerosis, Parkinson's disease, and Alzheimer's disease as brain diseases, but they do not so recognize schizophrenia and manic-depressive psychosis. It is perhaps worth mentioning that defenders of the psychiatric faith ceaselessly criticize me for holding that mental diseases are not (proven) brain diseases, but never—absolutely never—address the inconsistency between their views and the pathologists' views on schizophrenia. It seems to me not unreasonable, however, that psychiatrists ought to convince pathologists that schizophrenia is a brain disease before they take it upon themselves to tell the public that it is such a disease or try to silence those who disagree with them on this crucial issue.[20]

And what then, of Torrey's smaller heads, brains, and frontal lobes? Dr. Peter R. Breggin, M.D., a practicing psychiatrist, Harvard educated, formerly a teaching fellow at Harvard Medical School and full-time consultant with the National Institute of Mental Health, supplies an answer in his book, *Toxic Psychiatry*. Breggin, who subtitles his book *why therapy, empathy, and love must replace the drugs, electroshock, and biochemical theories of the "new psychiatry,"* writes:

Dozens of studies have . . . come out indicating
that neuroleptic-treated patients [patients
treated with antipsychotic drugs] have such
severe brain damage that it can be detected as
shrinkage of the brain on the newer radiology
techniques, such as the CT scan. . . . Many—but
not all—of my psychiatric colleagues view these
findings as the long-sought proof that schizophrenia is a brain disease. But the brain shrinkage cannot be due to schizophrenia. For decades
schizophrenia has been called a "functional disorder" precisely because it typically occurs in
the absence of any signs of organic brain disease. The recent finding that these individuals
have gross organic brain disease flies in the face
of this long-standing clinical experience. . . .
autopsy studies in the predrug era failed to find
any consistent gross pathology in the brains of
schizophrenics. Furthermore, we have animal
autopsy studies confirming that the neuroleptic
drugs do indeed damage the brain, even in
small, short-term doses.[21]

Breggin then details a report of a National Institute of
Mental Health study published in the New England
Journal of Medicine "led by Richard Suddath and including biological extremists E. Fuller Torrey and Daniel
Weinberger." The report describes a study of fifteen sets
of identical twins, in which "the diagnosed schizophrenic twin had shrinkage of brain tissue while the normal twin did not."[22] "Long before this particular research
project, Weinberger frequently had declared schizophrenia to be a proven biological disease. He would cite
brain-scan studies of patients without mentioning that
they already had been treated with electroshock and

with years of toxic drugs."[23] Torrey, who was chief investigator for the study, who "is a spokesman and the patron psychiatrist of NAMI [National Alliance for the Mentally Ill] . . . [and who] has supported NAMI's attacks on psychiatrists who disagree with NAMI and with him"[24] obviously had his own bias. "The report, and an accompanying editorial, claims to have proven the biological basis of schizophrenia. The investigators assume that the cause of the brain shrinkage is the presumed disease of schizophrenia and mention no other possibility in their lengthy abstract and introduction. Tucked toward the end of the article [however] was the admission that the results 'cannot rule out' treatment as the primary cause of the damage."[25] Breggin concludes, "The facts favor neuroleptic treatment, plus electroshock, as the cause of the brain shrinkage."[26]

These are indeed crucial issues. Using the diagnosis of brain disease, elevated to the level of canon by those luminaries of the "new psychiatry," Torrey, Weinberger, and Suddath, psychiatrists can treat schizophrenia as a disease is treated, as something to be eradicated. Many patients, however, do not feel that they are ill and do not wish to give up their so-called symptoms—they don't want to be treated. Torrey asserts this when he presents his case for enforced medication by stating that schizophrenics reject antipsychotic medication because they are unable to discern that they are ill, and because they do not think that anything at all is amiss.[27] I have already noted the position Torrey takes with reference to his patients, but the ramifications of this approach, which includes incarcerating an individual who does not want psychiatric help, who has not committed a crime, who has no intention of committing a crime, and who is not a danger to society in any way—are truly deplorable. This is not to say that schizophrenic individuals who are violent, or who are dangerous or criminal should not be dealt with in a manner to protect others. Most schizophrenics, however, are not a threat to their neighbors. Torrey himself affirms this when he writes that among the criminally insane it is the paranoid delusional subgroup of the schizophrenic that has caused people to think that schizophrenics are a danger to the community. He states that, as a matter of fact, this subgroup is comparatively quite small. Torrey asserts that schizophrenics, as a whole, present so little danger that he feels safer walking the corridors of a mental institution than walking around an inner city.[28]

Yet any non-criminal schizophrenic person who rejects the treatment proffered by Torrey may be forcibly institutionalized if Torrey considers it appropriate. And Torrey makes it abundantly clear, that as far as he is concerned, the rights of an individual are secondary to a psychiatrist's decision to commit that person for treatment. As would be expected, Torrey falls back upon his brain disease theory to support such an incursion into an individual's civil rights, arguing that a person with a diseased brain cannot make sound judgments in these matters. Torrey writes that the "concept" of brain disease is, in itself, reason enough to insist upon "the parens patriae role of the state"[29] so that people can be hospitalized involuntarily when it is considered requisite. He then recommends that once a person has been involuntarily committed to a psychiatric institution, that facility should be granted the right to impose obligatory treatment if required.[30]

Torrey does not stand alone, of course. This kind of empowerment is widely supported in the psychiatric community. In many states in America, a psychiatrist, regardless of an individual's personal wishes, may use a diagnosis of schizophrenia to institutionalize that individual and then may prescribe antipsychotic drugs, electroshock therapy (EST), and electroconvulsive therapy (ECT), frequently used in Europe, as well. Dr. Breggin, in *Toxic Psychiatry*, estimates that even if the rate of shock treatment doesn't increase, a million or more ECTs will be performed in the United States in the decade following the publication of his book (1991).[31] Psychiatrists may use any other treatment currently in vogue—not too long ago, frontal lobotomies were the treatment of the day. Today, chemical lobotomies are in the forefront of psychiatric treatments (see *Toxic Psychiatry*, chapter 3.)[32] The issue of diagnosis is crucial then, simply because none of these treatments, usually coercive (whether by mandate of law or by pressure of medical dictate), can be justified unless a patient has been labeled mentally ill—the term *ill* being applicable solely because brain disease is presumed to be the cause of mental illness.

It is clear that no hard and fast proofs exist to support the concept of schizophrenia as a brain disease. But the fact left standing is that the symptomatology of kundalini and schizophrenia, that is, all the mental productions described in both patient and kundalini accounts, are identical. Therefore, we have traced that symptomatology to its source, and that source is not brain disease. What remains, on the contrary, is the current of kundalini coursing through the brain and neurological system. This means that the symptoms attributred to schizophrenia are in actuality the symptoms that arise in categories 1 and 2 of the kundalini process as delineated at the close of chapter 3 of this text. (See pages 57–58.) I submit, therefore, that schizophrenia is a phase of the kundalini process—*schizophrenia is kundalini!*

If schizophrenia is kundalini and not a brain disease, then present methods of treatment must be reviewed. It is clear, in fact, from just a superficial glance, that clinical psychiatry has failed utterly in coping with the condition known as schizophrenia. Psychiatrists now view these symptoms as pathological, as something to be drugged, shocked, or locked up. Cure consists of having assured that the patient is ambulatory and more or less functional. A truly integrated personality is not even sought, and if it occurs it is by chance, a by-product of treatment. What *is* sought is to discharge patients from the hospital with their symptoms under control—that is the supreme goal clinical psychiatrists set for their patients.

In discussing twenty-four scientifically controlled studies using antipsychotic drugs, Torrey comments that every one of the studies showed that schizophrenics who received antipsychotic drug treatment were not as likely to be rehospitalized as patients who had not received the drugs.[33] This seems to be Torrey's only criterion of cure. What Torrey does not emphasize, though, is that many of these patients will require continued medication for years; and then there are the side effects, which are quite serious, including stiffness, loss of spontaneity, inability to speak without slurring, and hand and foot tremors.[34] Severe neurological symptoms can develop that include twitches, tics, debilitating muscle spasms, parkinsonism, and dementia. Other side effects include damage to the retina, heart abnormalities, liver damage, and even death. Yet Torrey is convinced that he is curing people. In *Surviving Schizophrenia*, he devotes thirty-four pages, almost the whole chapter titled "The Treatment of Schizophrenia," to symptom-suppressing drug treatments—the only actual treatment plan he offers in the entire book. In his chapter "What the Patient Needs," Torrey emphasizes his belief that drug therapy is the most important element in treating and restoring schizophrenics to health.[35] Diagnoses of brain disease are the *sine qua non* of drug treatment programs and of major funding for schizophrenic research. If, however, there is no scientific basis for defining schizophrenia as brain disease, which I have shown, and if we accept that schizophrenia is a certain stage of kundalini in progress, then there is no rationale for treating schizophrenic patients with antipsychotic drugs.

How then shall we proceed? For these patients do need help, not only physiologically, for proper diet and rest are extremely important, but also psychologically, particularly in terms of nurturance—they require solace, comfort, understanding, and insight into the kundalini process. Some present-day methods of treatment, for instance, psychoanalysis or psychotherapy, could still prove effective, if the therapy is geared toward comprehending and moving with the flow of the aroused kundalini. If, on the other hand, the only aim is the restoration of "functional" behavior, then such therapies will be no more helpful than they have been in the past. For the storms and fires of kundalini are far too fierce and powerful to be tamed by traditional psychotherapies. Dr. Torrey, as would be expected, makes a point of denigrating psychoanalysis and insight-oriented psychotherapy as ineffective treatments. He depicts Deborah Blau's descriptions of her symptoms in *I Never Promised You a Rose Garden* as fantastic. The psychotherapy that guided Blau to recovery is ridiculed by Torrey as having about as much chance of curing schizophrenia as it has of healing multiple sclerosis.

But Dr. John Weir Perry, the author of "Reconstitutive Process in the Psychopathology of the Self," previously referred to in chapter 5 writes:

> To learn at all satisfactorily what is going on in
> the inner preoccupations of a schizophrenic
> patient requires certain unavoidable conditions,

140 • Darrel Irving

chief of which is an intensely intimate relation of trust which takes weeks to establish. The imagery that is uppermost in importance to the patient is then brought to view only in the spirit of revealing the most personal and intimate of secrets. The patient is prone to feel distrust and, if there is a hint of any derogatory attitude toward these secrets, or any failure to regard them as meaningful, the veil may be quickly drawn over them despite any such futile measures as an external manner of friendly reassurance. The personal factor is apparently unavoidable; the patient will open up to one therapist and keep strictly closed to another. Even interest in and familiarity with the usage of symbols is not always sufficient to invite the patient to openness. My impression is that a mutual emotional field must be established in interaction with the patient by entering into a reciprocal intimacy of feeling with him. . . . Without this mutual emotional field, I doubt whether the process of reconstituting of the self does progress toward its goal.[36]

Torrey, obdurately closed to such considerations, would not be expected to agree. He states that Blau's case is more characteristic of hysteria (feigned or fantasized illness) than schizophrenia. This statement fits his conception that schizophrenia can only respond to antipsychotic drug therapy, since Blau did, in fact, become cured through psychoanalytic treatment. From the position Torrey takes here, and from his sole reliance on mind-numbing drugs as treatment for schizophrenia, it becomes obvious that Torrey, and the vast field of psychiatry of which he is representative, are on the wrong track with regard to schizophrenia. It is not just Dr. Torrey who is being singled out. All psychiatrists who insist that schizophrenia is a disease of the brain are being brought before the bar here. Perhaps they are not to blame, for as our observation of Torrey has shown, the bias and presumably the education and training of these doctors have all been geared toward drug treatment, not insightful therapy. Perry comments:

> I find, in teaching and supervising residents, that they are distinctly discouraged from paying any attention whatsoever to the inner mental content on their psychotic patient cases; it becomes almost axiomatic in this way that in their work of therapy they are not to let patients talk of their image-concerns, and are not to take these seriously as having meaningfulness. With this viewpoint, the unconscious as such is regularly and systematically overlooked.[37]

The pity is that these words were written in 1962, for it appears that such a viewpoint still prevails.

Today's clinical psychiatrists might well consider Perry's words, particularly when juxtaposed against Torrey's proclamation that from what has been discovered about the brains of schizophrenics, it should astonish no one to learn that psychotherapy that depends upon insight only makes schizophrenics sicker. According to Torrey, to apply insight-directed psychotherapy to schizophrenia is the same as flooding a city that has previously been devastated by a tornado.[38] Torrey follows this statement by calling up a similar analogy from a review titled, "The Adverse Effects of Intensive Treatment of Chronic Schizophrenia." The authors of this review write that insight-directed psychotherapies are "analogous to pouring boiling oil into wounds because they ignore the chronic schizophrenic's particular vulnerability to over-stimulating relationships, intense negative affects, and pressures for rapid change."[39]

Torrey and his colleagues obviously feel strongly about their advocacy. But when contrasted with Perry's approach, "What is needed . . . is enough contact to establish a relation of trust and openness between the patient and therapist in order to get the complete story of what the patient is concerned with delusionally,"[40] it seems clear that the Torrey camp has no real direction. Not possessing an insider's view of what the inside of the mind is like, nor the willingness to learn from those who can speak from such a vantage point, such as those who have gone through the kundalini experience, these psychiatrists have not approached the issue of so-called psychoses effectively. If these doctors, blinded by unsup-ported psychiatric beliefs about brain disease, do not have the vision to see the powerful writhings of the ser-pent kundalini mirrored in the transfigured eyes of the multitudes of patients who have appeared before them, how can they be entrusted with the mandate of finding a cure for schizophrenia?

• • • • •

Schizophrenia *is* kundalini. This means that the diagno-sis of schizophrenia has been and is being applied to individuals in whom kundalini has become active. Since schizophrenia is deemed incurable, these patients are given antipsychotic drugs in an attempt to suppress their symptoms. The objective of such a procedure, of course, is to return these persons quickly to their roles in society, whether or not they are fully functional. But as a result, the most dynamic feature of kundalini, the aspect that is actually curative, meaning the transcendent moment of bliss, of insight, the encounter with the divine, internal self that follows the lightning ascent of the kundalini current up the Sushumna has been blocked. The one thing that could have brought real relief, that could have made the entire experience truly healing and worthwhile, was doused with thorazine, stelazine, lithium, or a host of other chemicals designed to slay the kundalini serpent in its tracks. What a sense of futility it must engender in patients to find at the end of the anguish they have undergone in the schizophrenic experience that there is no release, no triumph, no sense of victory, not even true surcease, just continued medication and the prospect of further hospitalization. If these patients had been diagnosed as kundalini-activated individuals and given appropriate attention, however, the outcomes could have been very different. For as the four kundalini narratives have demonstrated, the prognosis for kundalini is extremely optimistic.

Kundalini does have the power to cleanse, heal, rejuvenate, and restore the psyche if given half a chance. This has been understood on occasion even by some in the psychiatric profession, including the celebrated Carl Gustav Jung. In fact, Jung considered the subject important enough to deliver a series of four kundalini lectures in Zurich. In the *Inner Reaches of Outer Space*, Joseph Campbell, who was steeped in the work of C. G. Jung and whose fascination with kundalini has already been noted in chapter 6, wrote "Kundalini yoga ... is not a game of 'as if' and make believe, but an actual experience of psychological absorption in a metaphysical ground of some kind, a morphogenetic field that has not yet, as far as I know, been scientifically recognized in the West except by C. G. Jung and lately, by the physicist Rupert Sheldrake. . . ."[41] Sheldrake, a Ph.D. Fellow of the Royal

Society in England and one of the world's foremost biologists, is representative of a new kind of scientist; he has moved beyond the mechanistic outlook of science to a viewpoint that sees the universe as mindful, purposeful, and evolving.

Jung, as we shall see, more than recognized kundalini. According to *Spring, An Annual of Archetypal Psychology and Jungian Thought*, which featured an editorial team headed by noted analyst, writer, and editor James Hillman, "Jung mentions Kundalini often in the Collected Works, and ... this system of images forms a basic part of his psychological language."[42] Jung became interested in kundalini after reading Sir John Woodroffe's *The Serpent Power*[43] shortly after the book's publication. The symbol of the serpent rising through the chakras helped Jung understand a patient whose symptoms had thoroughly perplexed him until then, and as a result, he was able to bring her case to a successful conclusion. In a paper titled "The Realities of Practical Psychotherapy," Jung details how he incorporated the Tantric ideas into the analysis, and writes, "To my astonishment, I found in [*The Serpent Power*] an explanation of all those things I had not understood in the patient's dreams and symptoms."[44]

In the four kundalini lectures, given in October and November of 1932, and which Jung called a "Psychological Commentary on Kundalini Yoga," he first makes some general observations about the psychology of Tantric Yoga, which he calls *mandala psychology*, and then draws some comparisons to the ideas of Plato, Kant, and St. Augustine. Jung then begins to introduce the chakras. These he presents as individual worlds, "new worlds of consciousness of natural growth, one above the other."[45] He says, "I have told you that my first discovery about the Kundalini Yoga was that these *chakras* really are concerned with what are called psychical localizations."[46] After some reflections on the Muladhara and Svadhisthana chakras Jung examines the kundalini itself. This he at first presents from a psychological standpoint and tells his audience:

> You see the Kundalini in psychological terms is that which makes you go on the greatest adventures. I say: "Oh, damn, why ever did I try such a thing?" But if I turn back, then the spirit of adventure goes out of my life and my life is nothing any longer; it has lost its flavour. It is this quest which makes life livable, and this is Kundalini, this is the divine urge.[47]

But Jung goes beyond the psychological in these lectures to include the metaphysical implications of the kundalini system as well. Summing up in the final lecture, having by then explored all the chakras, he states:

> Taken from the standpoint of the cosmic *chakra* system then, we can see that we are still very low down, that our culture is a culture in *muladhara*, only a personal culture where the Gods have not yet awakened from sleep. Therefore we have to awaken Kundalini in order to make clear to the individual spark of consciousness the light of the Gods. . . . in gaining a relation to the unconscious we undergo a development upward. To activate the unconscious means to awaken the divine, the *devi* Kundalini, to begin the development of the supra-personal within the individual in order to kindle the light of the Gods. Kundalini, which is to be awakened in the sleeping *muladhara* world, is the supra-per-

sonal, the non-ego, the totality of the psyche through which alone we can attain the higher *chakras* in a cosmic or metaphysical sense. . . .[48]

If a physician the stature of Jung, who has been called the veritable founder of analytical psychology, deemed kundalini worthy of serious consideration, perhaps some of today's students and professionals in the medical and scientific fields might be persuaded to investigate this enigmatic phenomenon as well. For what will be required in the future to redeem the promise of this morphogenetic field—to understand how the kundalini structure and process develop within the body—are new kinds of physicians and scientists. What is needed are healers and explorers emerging center stage who are thoughtful enough, and courageous enough, to turn away from mainstream ideas, principles, and practices in pursuit of unbiased answers to this momentous issue.

There are, in fact, such physicians and scientists out there now. They are the ones who are exploring the invisible, the paranormal, the unseen, who are trying to provide patient-oriented conditions where true and total healing can occur, and who have made an effort to truly understand the inner world of the mentally afflicted, not for the purpose of developing new drugs to zone patients out with a drug cure, but to aid them in an unremitting search for their lost selves. It is to these physicians and scientists and their capacity to think creatively that the future must look if real answers are to be found. Hopefully these practitioners will now take the lead in investigating kundalini and in creating a new atmosphere in medicine, in which the healing arts of kundalini are developed, studied, and elevated to the status of accepted medical practice and doctrine.

Chapter 8

The Thought
of Gopi Krishna

Only after his retirement from a lifelong position as a minor clerk in the Indian government in Kashmir did Gopi Krishna begin to disseminate his ideas about kundalini. He could have presented himself as a guru, a teacher, at any point in time, for he did possess wisdom, but that was not his primary interest. His purpose was to come to intellectual grips with kundalini and mystical knowledge so that others would have a basis for understanding altered states of mind. He felt that it was vitally important that serious scientific investigation be undertaken into the kundalini phenomenon.

Gopi Krishna knew right from the start that the stream of light that came roaring like a waterfall into his brain was kundalini. In India, kundalini is known among religious seekers, so there was some basis from which to understand what had happened. Even so, kundalini is still regarded as a mysterious phenomenon, even in India, and Gopi Krishna knew very little about the subject. It had never occurred to him that kundalini was actually a biological process intrinsic to every human being. This he came to realize later, as the result of his own personal experience. For he could actually observe the inward motion of kundalini as it operated upon the

148 • Darrel Irving

organs and internal structures of his own body. Eventually he would assert that kundalini was a mechanism of evolution by which the entire human race could and would ultimately be elevated to a new plane. This interest in the mechanics of kundalini pervades his work and led him to explore the biological aspects of kundalini as few before him have done. In *Kundalini—The Secret of Yoga*, for example, he analyzes in detail the physiology of the cerebrospinal system—the spinal cord, vertebral column, brain, prevertebral and vertebral ganglia, the autonomic nervous system, the vagus nerve, which aligns both sides of the spinal column, etc.—as this system applies to kundalini. He states that the spinal cord, with the reproductive equipment at one end and the brain at the other end, is the largest repository of prana, the vital life-force, in the body. He also asserts that in the cerebrospinal system are located all the mechanisms of kundalini, which is to say, the evolutionary mechanism or system.

Gopi Krishna writes that it is no accident that the reproductive and the evolutionary (kundalini) systems exist in such close proximity. For the "activity of the nervous system, in the evolutionary as well as in the reproductive sphere, lies in extracting from the mass of tissue surrounding every nerve fibre an extremely subtle but highly potent essence [prana] that may well be designated as concentrated life force. . . ."[1] This concentrated life force filters into the various nerves and nerve clusters lining various organs and down into the reproductive system at the bottom of the spinal column, where it vitalizes the sex cells, transmitting fertility to the ovum and to the spermatozoon. But in men and women in whom this prana exists to a comparatively greater degree, it can, instead of dissipating in procreational activity, become a stream that can irrigate, develop, and irradiate the brain, leading to a transformation in consciousness. This is actually a process in which the sexual energy is reversed; for the prana, the concentrated life force, instead of flowing downward and outward as it usually does, flows inward and upward. In other words, the activity of the reproductive system has been reversed. Here, according to Gopi Krishna, is how it works: the reproductive apparatus reacts upon itself in a manner so as to use its own energy to intensify its activity. This heightened activity produces a "highly increased aggregate of genital secretions and essences."[2] The reproductive system now becomes a transfer center in which these secretions and essences are transformed into an even more powerful nerve energy. This then courses upward into the brain, resulting in heightened awareness, increased psychic ability, and altered states of consciousness.[3]

This reversal of the sex energy, called *Urdhvareta* in Sanskrit, is the cornerstone of Gopi Krishna's doctrine. He emphasizes that this process can occur in both men and women, and he credits all genius, whether of the past or present, to this process of biological transformation. Gopi Krishna emphasized that the entire process was the result of an activated kundalini.[4] Here Gopi Krishna elaborates further:

The whole of our body is filled with a very fine biochemical essence which I call the biological prana. . . . This prana is concentrated in the sex-energy. Normally the sex energy is used for procreative purposes, but nature has designed it for evolutionary purposes also. . . . As the evolutionary mechanism, it sends a fine stream of a very potent nerve-energy into the brain and another stream into the sexual regions. . . .[5]

At this point one feels compelled to ask if Gopi Krishna is making the point that the reversal of the sexual energy and the arousal of kundalini are one and the same thing. In fact, Gopi Krishna does affirm this. "By the arousal of Kundalini we mean the reversal of the reproductive system and its functioning more as an evolutionary than as a reproductive mechanism."[6]

Gopi Krishna informs his readers that this idea dates back to the ancient teachings. He does not take the reversal of the sexual energy on faith just because it is written in the old treatises, however, for he was able to discern this process occurring in his own body: "a new type of force was now racing through my system connected unmistakably with the sexual parts, which also seemed to have developed a new kind of activity not perceptible before."[7] In this process, Gopi Krishna says, the sexual seed is sublimated to form an integral part of the radiant energy—kundalini energy—that is transmitted through the spinal cord into the brain.

It is important to understand that Gopi Krishna was not merely "visualizing" this process—he was actually seeing it internally through a kind of penetrating inner sight he had acquired as the result of the activated kundalini. In fact, Gopi Krishna was able to see the kundalini energy functioning in all areas of the body, not just in the cerebrospinal system:

> . . . the luminous current was acting with full knowledge of the task it had to perform. . . . The living fire, invisible to everyone else, darted here and there as if guided unerringly by a master-mind which knew the position of each vein and artery and each nerve fibre, and decided instantaneously what it had to do at the least sign of a hitch or disturbance in any organ. With

marvellous agility it raced from one spot to
another, exciting this organ to greater activity,
slowing down another, causing a greater or
lesser flow of this secretion or that, stimulating
the heart and liver, bringing about countless
functional and organic changes in the innumerable cells, blood vessels, nerve fibres, and other
tissues . . .[8]

Gene Kieffer, in his treatise *The Secret of Kundalini*, points
out that confusion exists as to how the reversal of the sexual energy shall occur. One of the prevalent ideas in
Tantric practices about how to achieve this reversal is the
withholding of orgasm at the crucial moment. Mr. Kieffer
elaborates on this idea by quoting from *The Secret of the
Golden Flower*, the ancient Chinese Book of Life. Kieffer
first quotes from the introduction by Charles San, who
writes: "The one essential key to opening the Golden
Flower is *the sexual energy of the individual*, which must be
aroused and converted into spiritual force. The same
process is found in Hindu Yoga under the name of 'Kundalini'. . . ."[9] In a passage headed "The Backward-Flowing Method," Kieffer explores *The Secret of the Golden
Flower* further:

Now if one closes the eyes and, reversing the
glance, directs it inward and looks at the room
of the ancestors, that is the backward-flowing
method. The power of the kidneys is under the
water sign. When the instincts are stirred, it
runs downward, is directed outward, and creates children. If, in the moment of release, it is
not allowed to flow outward but is led back by
the force of thought so that it penetrates the cru-
cible of the creative and refreshes heart and

body and nourishes them, that also is the backward-flowing method. Therefore it is said: The
meaning of the Elixir of Life depends entirely on
the backward-flowing method.[10]

Kieffer says: "The meaning should have been clear. A
man should abstain from ejaculation at the time of
orgasm in order to be able to 'circulate the Light.' How
this seemingly simply act is to be achieved, however, is
not explained but left to the guru to tell his disciple."[11]

Here Mr. Kieffer arrives at the heart of the confusion—how this "seemingly simple act" shall be
approached. For Gopi Krishna is not advocating techniques of activating kundalini such as Tantra-Asana or
any similar occult practices when he describes the reversal
of the sexual energy; rather, he is merely depicting a biological process. It may also be noted that *The Secret of the
Golden Flower* ignores the female perspective with regard
to this issue, and Gopi Krishna clearly attributes this
process to both women and men. The process Gopi
Krishna is describing can be aided but not by a kind of sexual activity that goes contrary to nature, such as withholding orgasm. On the contrary, Gopi Krishna is saying
that a kind of virtuousness is required, not celibacy per se,
but a highly developed character, with thoughts chaste
and pure, and without undue emphasis on the sexual
impulse. Author Kieffer, who, if anybody, could be said to
have been a disciple of Gopi Krishna, and who knows his
thought well, confirms that this was Gopi Krishna's position. Gopi Krishna does not infer any connection at all
between sexual activity and kundalini arousal. Sexual
practices decidedly are not the way.

At the opposite end of the spectrum is sexual absti-
nence. Gopi Krishna does not recommend this either. In
his book, *The Awakening of Kundalini*, Gopi Krishna

discusses the issue of celibacy with his editor, Gene Kieffer. In the following dialogue, Gopi Krishna has just stated that with the arousal of kundalini the reproductive system is reversed and functions more as an evolutionary than as a reproductive mechanism:

> **Gene K:** Is that the reason many religions advocated celibacy?
>
> **Gopi K:** There must be some cogent reason for it. . . . Unless sexual energy is needed in some way for spiritual disciplines, why should . . . any spiritual teacher recommend celibacy as a method of reaching God?
>
> **Gene K:** To conserve the energy?
>
> **Gopi K:** Yes. . . . Unless it has a direct effect in leading to higher states of consciousness why should any spiritual teacher advocate celibacy?
>
> **Gene K:** In the West, we've always associated sexual activities, at least in the past, with immorality. We had no idea that sexual energy might have had another use.
>
> **Gopi K:** Well, sometimes this idea appears to be very comic and sometimes very tragic. I cannot say what is the frame of mind of one who calls the sexual act a sin when he owes his existence to this act.
>
> **Gene K:** But we've been taught, at least up until the last few decades, that this is true enough; but then it shouldn't be used for any other purpose, especially not for gratification of our sensual desires—only for the reproductive process, and that's all.

> **Gopi K:** Even admitting that, is the Creator or
> God of such limited intelligence that he should
> build man in such a way that the sexual urge is
> the most awful impulse in him, attended with
> such an intense pleasure, and then rule that he
> is not to touch it?[12]

It is important to be very clear about the issue of celibacy
with regard to kundalini. As Mr. Kieffer has pointed out
in one of his queries, sexuality has often been associated
with immorality. This is particularly noticeable in the
spiritual disciplines, where gurus and enlightened masters are frequently expected to have controlled their sexual impulses under the presumption that celibacy is the
way to enlightenment. Consequently, many spiritual
leaders and guides have used celibacy as a mantle of
saintliness. At the end of their studies, their pilgrimage,
their spiritual odyssey, they pronounce that they have
experienced *nirvakalpa samadhi*, that is, that they have
reached ultimate enlightenment. They then take on a
flock of disciples whom they initiate into a new round of
celibacy, thus assuring the continuation of "saintliness"
in the future.

Surely, though, it is an error to equate cosmic consciousness with saintliness. In the second interview
appearing in chapter 10 of this book, "The Sovereignty of
Mystical Experience," Gopi Krishna asserts that he is
only a normal human being, with all the frailties and
vanities common to human nature. He then points out
that he does reside in "the transcendental state of consciousness . . . [but that it] is only a more extended
dimension of the perceptual faculty toward which
mankind is evolving. . . ."[13] Hopefully the concept that
saintliness leads to enlightenment will fall by the way-
side in coming years and the transcendental experience,

or cosmic consciousness, will be seen for what it really is—the fulfillment of human potential and the elevation of mind and spirit to a new level of capacity.

In *The Awakening of Kundalini*, Gopi Krishna makes it abundantly clear that celibacy is not necessary for heightened development of the spiritual process. He points out that the hundreds of inspired sages of the Upanishads were all married with children. Mr. Kieffer confirms this in *The Secret of Kundalini*. "In India there are records [showing that from] 1000 B.C. to 500 B.C.—there were 300 men who had achieved Illumination and who left their testimonies. Of these, 298 were married. Some had more than one wife!"[14] In fact, celibacy may be counterproductive, for it is not a natural way of life. Gopi Krishna emphasizes that if the attainment of a higher state of consciousness is the goal of nature, it would not make sense for men and women to go against the grain of the strong impulses and instincts that nature has implanted in them to ensure the survival of the species. Just when human beings are about to reach a higher plane of consciousness, they would be abandoning the strong urges that led them to seek the goal.

Gopi Krishna stresses that spiritual evolution should be a natural process. Methods that are unnatural cannot lead to what he calls a "healthy consummation."[15] A normal, healthy, and moderate life is essential, free from immoderate ambitions and abnormal lusts. People must lead lives that bring internal peace, and as much as possible, a life of selfless service to others, seeking peace and joy for oneself and striving to be a "source of solace and happiness for others."[16]

It is interesting to note that although Gopi Krishna wrote, discussed, and talked a great deal about kundalini, he did not teach it per se, for he believed that individuals are different and that what works for one person may be harmful to another. He did acknowledge, however, that transformation can be achieved by means of mental or physical exercises, and just before he died, he finally did write a small book titled *The Way to Self-Knowledge*, offering helpful hints on how to safely awaken the serpent power.[17] Gopi Krishna remarked that if the existence of an evolutionary mechanism in the body were going to be conceded, then it must also be conceded that it can be activated by certain kinds of stimuli, coming either from "the outside world," or from a person's "freely acting mind."[18] He insisted, though, that in every case transcendence was dependent upon kundalini.

With regard to kundalini practices, Gopi Krishna strongly admonishes against forced arousal through violent and forcible methods, for this can cause a morbid awakening wherein the kundalini rises up the ida or pingala channel instead of the Sushumna, or partly through one of these channels and the Sushumna. He warns of grave consequences that can threaten the life and sanity of any man or woman unfortunate enough to attempt this. These consequences have already been examined in the preceding chapters, and it is inconceivable that anyone would undergo that kind of trauma voluntarily.

How then, shall a student of kundalini proceed? Gopi Krishna did not disapprove of the study of various Yogic disciplines or certain unspecified occult or religious practices. He said, "Yoga, or occult practice tends to stir up *kundalini* . . . The generally expressed view that in Raja-Yoga, Bakhti-Yoga, Karma-Yoga, or Jnana-Yoga, or in other forms of religious striving, *kundalini* is not awakened is not correct."[19] He then emphasizes that without some natural mechanism already present in the body capable of being activated by such exercises, all such efforts could only result in failure. Gopi Krishna punctuates these statements with a quote from Swami

Vivekananda. "Whenever there is any manifestation of what is ordinarily called supernatural power or wisdom there must have been a little current of *kundalini*, which found its way into the *susumna*."[20]

Gopi Krishna offers no advice on how to activate kundalini. The inference seems to be that we must each find our own answer, that what is important is to try to perceive one's own place in the grand cosmic scheme of life and to then play that role with conviction, dedication, reverence, and love in the heart. Ultimately, illumination is in the cards for everyone in this lifetime or another, and kundalini may at this very moment be gathering energy, right around the corner, as Gopi Krishna, Krishnamurti, Dr. Motoyama, and I each discovered. We all had a difficult crossing, but we all made it, and much can be learned from our transit.

Kundalini will always come unexpectedly. It may come during meditation, as it happened to Gopi Krishna and Dr. Motoyama, with a painful lump on the nape of the neck, as experienced by Krishnamurti, or as it came to me, with a primordial hum and a lump appearing on the nape of my neck during a drug trip. I was extremely lucky to escape the consequences previously described by Gopi Krishna, for I walked a tightwire across the fires of an inferno, without a balance beam, without any preparation, without any idea of how to proceed once I found myself up there. In *The Stormy Search for the Self*, coauthor Christina Grof describes an initial kundalini awakening that occurred during the birth of her first child.

> After only a few hours of labor, my son was suddenly and rapidly making his way into the world as . . . the people around me encouraged me to "push . . . push . . ." I felt an abrupt snap

somewhere inside of me as powerful and unfamiliar energies were released unexpectedly and
began streaming through my body. I started
to shake uncontrollably. Enormous electrical
tremors coursed from my toes up my legs and
spine to the top of my head. Brilliant mosaics of
white light exploded in my head, and instead of
continuing the Lamaze panting, I felt strange,
involuntary breathing rhythms taking over.

It was as though I had just been hit by some
miraculous but frightening force, and I was both
excited and terrified. . . .[21]

The kundalini subsided after an injection of morphine
following the delivery. But in this incident, as in the four
kundalini narratives, one specific common denominator
should be noted—no one was sufficiently prepared spiritually, mentally, or physically. If anything, these experiences point to the need to prepare oneself for spiritual
awakenings through reading, understanding, self-explo-
ration, and contemplation on the nature of Self and God.

Every story described in this text thus far is riven
with the most awesome internal forces. Is kundalini,
then, always accompanied by such agitation? Such
stress? Are there no reported instances of gradual, gentle
awakening? Gopi Krishna indicates, in fact, that a pleasant awakening is natural. The reason for the preponder-
ance of difficult "births" is that people have not equipped
their bodies and minds to handle the unleashing of such
potent energies.

Gopi Krishna says, in fact, that a "normal awakening
does not arouse intense heat. There is only a pleasant sensation of warmth, beginning from the *muladhara* and
spreading to the whole of the body. . . ."[22] He then
informs his readers that the view of the ancient writers

on kundalini was that the purpose of heat was to aid the digestive system which is why heat is found in the umbilical center—the Manipura chakra. It is this digestive heat that creates the sense of a great fire. Naturally, if one's digestive tract is functioning poorly, this fire could become a conflagration. Gopi Krishna describes it thus: "the awakening of the serpent power in the umbilical region is revealed by the sensation of a great fire. In fact, the ascent of *kundalini* is like the pouring of liquid flame into the various *cakras* and finally into the cranium. It may also resemble the brilliant luster shed by a prolonged flash of lightning, accompanied by noises like thunder."[23] Gopi Krishna goes on to say that descriptions of a blazing fire, lightning, or burning heat were not included in the ancient texts for this would have introduced an ominous feature into the accounts. On the contrary, kundalini was described as a cool, refreshing luster. Repeated mention of the moon in the Sahasrara chakra supports the contention that benign awakenings are a natural part of the process.

The ancient books on Kundalini-Yoga also contained accounts of individuals in whom kundalini had been active since birth. Gopi Krishna reports, "Almost all of those who had this spiritual power center naturally active from birth, not being aware of the biological nature of the force at work in their bodies, usually attributed all manifestations and developments to divine favor, and where things went wrong to satanic or demonic influences. . . . In the case of those in whom the awakening occurred through prolonged effort, the Grace of God or the favor of the divine Shakti provided the answer. . . ."[24]

This is not surprising. All civilizations of the past responded similarly to phenomena they could not explain. There probably always have been both benign and malignant kundalini awakenings. But the need to lay the proper groundwork cannot be overemphasized, so that the kundalini experience can be propitious. Gopi Krishna says, "In dealing with *kundalini* we deal with a divine power center in man designed to lead him to a knowledge of his own immortal, superearthly nature by a process of sifting, purification, and remodeling. . . . There must, therefore, be a certain state of preparedness and maturity, both mental and physical, in all those in whom the self-launched efforts terminate in success."[25]

Gopi Krishna's outlook is essentially optimistic and he strikes a note of hope for kundalini in the future:

> Even with all these difficulties the number of those in whom the awakening, whether present from birth or resulting from practice, was successful in different parts of the world is surprisingly large. With the knowledge now available and the rapid rate of progress in almost all directions, the proportion of success is now likely to be a hundred times greater, if this divine quest is earnestly taken up by the luminaries of this age.[26]

Chapter 9

Kundalini
and Hallucinogens

Hallucinogens—including drugs such as LSD, fungus such as psilocybin, and herbs, cacti, or plants such as marijuana, peyote, mescaline, and opium—have played a role in the history of metaphysical rites and practices. In fact, hallucinogens have been used from earliest times, by both primitive and sophisticated cultures, from the mushrooms of Mexican Indians to the psychedelic potions of 20th-century European and American pop cultures. Hallucinogens have served as keys to the same dominions of the unconscious, the same internal territories, marvelous or demoniacal, that have been described in mystical experience. Both the mystic and the hallucinogenic user describe far provinces of another dimension—kingdoms of the mind governed by factors beyond all previous experience and garnished by meanings they could hardly fathom.

In the two interviews following this chapter, Gopi Krishna remarks that the visions of light, sounds, bizarre experiences, or altered states of awareness induced through drug use are unlike the mystical experience. Hallucinogenic use differs vastly from standard drug use, however, the most obvious difference being that hallucinogens are often used in a religious context. More importantly, hallucinogens can lead to higher states of consciousness; for both the mystical and hallucinogenic experience transpire on the same mental plane, deep inside the mind.

Most individuals who have had an experience of kundalini would probably not recommend the use of hallucinogens to awaken this powerful energy. This probably reflects the same position taken toward hallucinogens by most spiritual leaders throughout the world. I am in agreement with this viewpoint. For one thing it is impossible just by taking a drug to recreate another person's experience, for example, the events described by Gopi Krishna. Those were unique to Gopi Krishna, based upon his personality, his disposition, and all the individual character traits that belonged to him alone. Those experiences will never recur. Second, the waters I have described throughout this text, so often dark, murky, and seething, can be dangerous and terrifying. No one who fully understands what may be in store would voluntarily dive into such fearsome depths. There are no thrills there, and for the uninitiated, the spiritually unprepared, the burning fires of a private hell may be waiting. Gopi Krishna was right about the dangers of forcing the arousal of kundalini, which hallucinogens can do, and his warnings of dire consequences should be taken very seriously.

Hallucinogenic substances do have the power to draw the hidden levels of the mind into focus—so can a spontaneous chemical reaction within the body, i.e., a spontaneous increase in prana, as happens in meditation and schizophrenia. Once this process has been triggered, and the barrier separating the conscious from the unconscious has receded, the sage, the user of hallucinogens, and the schizophrenic all find themselves swimming in the same waters. Joseph Campbell writes:

> The LSD phenomenon . . . is an intentionally achieved schizophrenia, with the expectation of a spontaneous remission—which, however, does not always follow. Yoga, too, is an intentional schizophrenia: one breaks away from the world, plunging inward, and the ranges of vision experienced are in fact the same as those of a psychosis. But what, then, is the difference? What is the difference between a psychotic or LSD experience and a yogic, or mystical? The plunges are all into the same deep inward sea; of that there can be no doubt. The symbolic figures encountered are in many instances identical. . . .[1]

The difference is that the sage knows how to rise to the surface where the sun is bright and warm, where there is a view of tropical islands and the foaming surf crashing onto soft, powdered beaches; the sage can go ashore to the warmth of hearth and home. But the user of hallucinogens who has aroused the kundalini negatively and the schizophrenic find themselves far from shore in deep, stormy waters. They are sinking, and no matter how they struggle, they sink only deeper, not knowing up from down—lost at sea.

Joseph Campbell continues his account with a similar analogy. He writes, "The difference—to put it sharply—is equivalent simply to that between a diver who can swim and one who cannot. The mystic, endowed with native talents for this sort of thing and following, stage by stage, the instruction of a master, enters the waters and finds he can swim; whereas the schizophrenic, unprepared, unguided, and ungifted, has fallen or has intentionally plunged, and is drowning. Can he be saved? If a line is thrown to him, will he grab it?"[2] For most users of hallucinogens the answer is probably yes. But some may not be so lucky, for as Campbell has pointed out, spontaneous remission does not always follow.

I myself am grateful to have had the kundalini experience. Yet, I cannot bring myself to sing the praises of hallucinogenic drugs. Reflecting upon my experience, I recall realizing a few days after my own use of LSD, how confusing and terrifying schizophrenia would be if it were precipitated not by an hallucinogenic substance, but spontaneously, and in someone who had no mystical background or frame of reference from which to understand a world that had gone suddenly topsy-turvy. Such a person would most certainly end up confined to a mental institution. If my kundalini had not awakened so positively, and if I had not been vouchsafed a spontaneous remission of the effects of the drug I had taken, I too might have made the mistake of turning to psychiatry to guide me through the ordeal. And we have seen that psychiatry has yet to show that it has acquired even a superficial understanding of altered states of mind. The well-meaning doctors would have drugged me up and would have denied me the spiritual experience of a lifetime.

The hallucinogenic experience is for real, but I cannot recommend it insofar as kundalini is concerned. For those interested in awakening kundalini, I do recommend the counsel of masters like Gopi Krishna, Jiddu Krishnamurti, or Dr. Motoyama. Otherwise, it is advisable to become well grounded in the subject, to become physically healthy through proper diet and exercise, and to learn how to meditate according to those who have actually aroused the kundalini successfully. More important than anything else, though, is to live a full and happy life, to uncover the spirit of generosity and love within oneself, to find out how to exorcise rage and hatred, and to learn how to think freely and independently. With such skills as these, it may be possible not only to activate the kundalini, but to raise the fiery force benignly.

The driving motivation when I began this text was simply to tell my own story of what kundalini is. Second to this was my belief that kundalini can help light the way as civilization turns the corner into a new century, into what hopefully will be a more enlightened era. In the telling, as I became better acquainted with the ideas of Gopi Krishna (who is interviewed in the next chapter) I began to see the importance of his body of thought, not so much on a one-to-one basis, that is, in teaching others how to reach enlightenment as so many of the illuminati do, but rather in a more universal sense; for instance, his ideas on the biological basis of kundalini; his emphasis on the need for scientific research to prove the existence of kundalini; his ideas on the chakras and the reversal of the sexual energy, all of which remains to be proven, to be sure, and his acceptance of that, his insistence that all of his ideas, too, must be investigated scientifically. Then there is his rejection of saintliness and celibacy as ingredients of spirituality; his vision of the future, with kundalini as the key to the evolutionary mechanism; his sense of the vastness of God; and his vision of the infinite possibilities inherent in the evolutionary procession of humankind across the coming ages. In other words, his vision of the infinite possibilities for you and me.

Gopi Krishna may well represent the apotheosis of the kundalini experience as it has been recorded in contemporary times. The fact that he could see the kundalini current operating in his own body on a daily basis lends gravity to every word he spoke, whether or not his ideas about the process are ultimately proven right or wrong. He surely must be given an objective hearing, for this is a man whose life story comprises one of the most remarkable tales of our time.

Chapter 10

Gopi Krishna on Kundalini and the Sovereignty of Mystical Experience

Interviewed by Gene Kieffer

Gene Kieffer is one of the foremost leaders in the study, exploration, and research into kundalini, and was a close friend and associate of Gopi Krishna from 1970, when they first met, until Gopi Krishna's death in July 1984. A Des Moines, Iowa, businessman, Mr. Kieffer moved to New York City in 1969 to work for world peace. He is currently the director of the Kundalini Research Foundation, Ltd., which he founded in 1970 at Gopi Krishna's request. He is a member of the Academy of Religion and Psychical Research, and serves on the Board of Directors of the Temple of Understanding, an organization devoted to promoting dialogue among the religions of the world. Mr. Kieffer has written voluminously about kundalini and is the editor of the book *The Awakening of Kundulini*, by Gopi Krishna (published by E. P. Dutton) and *Kundalini for the New Age: Selected Writings of Gopi Krishna*, published by Bantam Books.

The following interview took place in 1983 at Gopi Krishna's home in Dehra Dun, a small city in the foothills of the Himalayas, about 250 miles north of New Delhi. This interview was selected from the files of the Kundalini Research Foundation, Ltd., and originally appeared in *Yoga Journal*, November/December, 1983.

ON KUNDALINI

Gene Kieffer: If we accept the hypothesis that kundalini is the psycho-physiological mechanism that can lead to higher states of consciousness, how can a person go about preparing himself for the arousal or awakening of this power?

Gopi Krishna: Kundalini is certainly the psycho-physiological mechanism responsible for higher consciousness, but it is not a mechanism in the same sense that a computer is. This mechanism is operated by an energy which also operates our brain. It is known as *prana* in the Indian tradition, and it is this energy which science has still to know about . . . The only way to locate and know about this energy is by inner observation.

Kundalini must awaken by itself. Even when we start the practices, it is by an impulse from within. Mind is a stuff, and our fancies, our dreams, our thinking, our reasoning are made of this stuff. And this stuff is completely imperceptible to our senses. We only use a fragment of this mind-stuff which surrounds us. A good part of it remains hidden behind the scenes, operating our body and acting to keep us alive with our day-to-day existence.

Gene Kieffer: What motivates us to want to raise our consciousness?

Gopi Krishna: When we start a spiritual practice, we feel an urge to do it. We feel an urge to know ourselves or to fathom the mystery of existence. It comes from kundalini itself. It is for this reason that, in the Indian tradition, kundalini has been treated as the architect. She is the queen of our body. We are but projections which she sends out as the *jiva*, the imprisoned fragment of the Absolute. We are an imprisoned ray of light from a divine sun. And this imprisoned ray of light is held captive by this all-intelligent life energy, known as *prana shakti*.

This urge to practice yoga comes from kundalini. In many people in whom this urge occurs there also occurs a desire for self-perfection. They withdraw from the world or they want to do good actions, or to do noble deeds. They want to be self-sacrificing. They feel more compassion for others. These have been the characteristics of most of the mystics born in the world. So you can see a link, a physiological link, in all that I say.

A mind devoted to higher consciousness must withdraw itself, to some extent, from the worldly struggle. In fact, this present civilization and all its amenities with which science is providing us is also nature's effort to provide more leisure for man so that he is able to withdraw himself, partially, from the worldly struggle in order to devote his mind to reaching a higher state of consciousness. It is a means to an end, but we are treating it as an end in itself and using it for multiple comforts of our body.

Human evolution, which is proceeding because of this psycho-somatic mechanism, is also proceeding further and further in science, philosophy, psychology, art, etc., in order to make of us better human beings, with more facilities and amenities—with also more knowledge of the nervous system and the brain—so that we may be able to devote more time to the search after God.

Gene Kieffer: Then there are specific practices that can activate this mechanism and accelerate the process of evolution?

Gopi Krishna: Now, this is another point. We must ask ourselves, how has the race progressed to this state of knowledge and culture so far? If we look very attentively, we will find that the only secret, the only method by which man has progressed until now is by mental application on a particular subject.

People with an urge for knowledge of the stars used to gaze at the sky for hours. People with an urge for treating diseases used to devote their mind to the exploration of drugs and herbs and diseases of the body. It will be found universally that whatever knowledge man has gained so far has come through the application of his mind and intellect, through study and concentration.

Gene Kieffer: Then concentration is the natural method for reaching higher knowledge?

Gopi Krishna: Yes, the same concentration for gaining knowledge and experience of the world also applies to reaching the higher states of consciousness. All the practices for attainment of higher awareness have meditation as a cardinal exercise. It is because concentration is the natural method for evolution of the brain. Ultimately, what happens is that with prolonged concentration, a certain region in the brain wakes up. That is the awakening of kundalini.

Gene Kieffer: What about the dormant energy at the base of the spine?

Gopi Krishna: Along with the awakening of that center in the brain a new form of energy starts to pour into the head. It comes from the reproductive essences—transformed into what is known as *ojas*—and floods the brain. The new consciousness which results is not something imaginary; it has a concrete reality.

Gene Kieffer: Many scientists have taken this to be simply a symbolic concept, having no reality in the physical body. But you believe it is physical as well as subjective?

Gopi Krishna: I am talking about something which has a tradition extending to 5,000 years, corroborated by hundreds of thousands of yogis and also recorded in thousands of books. I am not concerned with what the scientists say, because at this moment they are completely lacking in real knowledge about the brain and the nervous system. The time is near, now, when they will have to accept this position.

Gene Kieffer: If they do accept the position, it will have to be empirically verifiable.

Gopi Krishna: They will have to accept it because the experiments which I am proposing will ultimately show that what I am saying is correct; that under certain conditions, a dormant center in the brain can leap to activity. They already have the evidence in the case of geniuses, and even in the case of mediums and certain categories of the mentally afflicted. But since instruments to record the subtle energies working in the body are not yet available, they are not able to locate the mechanism which I am describing. The time is near, however. It won't take long to reach a state where scientists will virtually be able to see the operation of this energy.

Gene Kieffer: The general impression prevailing is that man has reached the highest state of his existence and that intellect is all that is needed to live.

Gopi Krishna: This is not a correct attitude of the mind. All religious revelation lays stress on cardinal virtues, on morality, on nobility of character, on truthfulness, on compassion, on non-violence, on fellow-feeling and on neighborly love. These qualities, however, do not fit in the scientific concept of a struggle for existence.

In fact, the struggle for existence—or survival of the fittest—means a disregard for another's feelings, which is a quality we see in animals. But when we come to man, we see the beginning of a conscience or a moral sense. Whatever the reason, man believes in neighborly love, in truth, honesty, compassion. Whether it is due to religious teaching, social pressures, or man's own instinctive development, the fact remains that humanity as a whole believes in the cardinal virtues in human character.

All our jurisprudence and all our ideologies are based on this fact. It is because man is reaching toward a consciousness, reaching toward a state of mind, where above everything else he needs peace, tranquility and security. Aggression and violence will always lead to distraction and disturbance. You can only look to the bottom of a pool when the surface is unruffled. For this purpose, it is essential that man should live a moral life. There is a barrier, imposed by nature, for anyone who does not lead a moral life, forbidding him from proceeding further. If he forces his way, the result is what we see in the lunatic asylums everywhere.

Gene Kieffer: This barrier, then, is what prevents anyone from actually awakening kundalini successfully?

Gopi Krishna: It doesn't only hinder the awakening of kundalini, but it will make human life impossible. The more our intelligence grows, the more should human life, individually and collectively, be ruled by moral laws. If it isn't, man will annihilate himself. Imagine what it would be like if immoral people came into power in every country that has nuclear arms.

Gene Kieffer: Do you see any way of escaping annihilation?

Gopi Krishna: It is absolutely imperative for human beings to become more and more moral as we progress in our intellectual achievements, because slowly we are gaining control over the most terrible forces of nature, and in the hands of a lustful man, who has no self-discipline, humanity will always remain in danger of its life. You cannot combine an immoral humanity with the power it has gained over the forces of nature, even up to this time. If we gain control over the psychic forces—the subtle forces of nature—then our moral advancement becomes even more imperative. We will not be able to survive. Therefore, it doesn't rest with you or me, whether we should be moral or should not be moral; it is an imperative which we have to obey.

I don't say that we should be perfect. I say that we should live a reasonably moderate life. I have also done the same. I am not an angel or a saint. I have lived a moderately normal life, and I have succeeded. Nature doesn't demand of men what is impossible but what is possible and within his own control. There is no need for austerity, penance, self-mortification, fasting, or for giving up any pleasure of the earth.

Gene Kieffer: If a person, whether practicing Yoga or not, happens to have a momentary flash of illumination, does that leave him or her permanently changed?

Gopi Krishna: It should. The experience is so staggering that it should. But then it should be a genuine flash, not just something imaginary, or fanciful, or like a drug experience. If it is not just a visionary experience, induced by passive types of meditation or drugs, it should leave a permanent mark.

Gene Kieffer: Many of us have been led to think that mystical experience is only subjective. What one might think is genuine may be only genuine for him, and what I experience is only genuine for me. The experience may not be the same. You claim that it is not only a subjective experience, but that it can be objectively verified, also.

Gopi Krishna: Thinking is thinking. It may differ on various aspects, but there is some underlying homogeneity in human consciousness. Can we suppose that in the higher states of consciousness there is utter confusion and that everyone can have what he thinks is mystical experience? There must be some underlying uniformity there also, and to know what it is we have only to read and study the thousands of books that record the experience of these mystics. The earliest are the *Upanishads*. They can all provide us with a model of what a mystical experience actually is.

Gene Kieffer: How can the mystical experience be conveyed to others?

Gopi Krishna: One of the characteristics of genuine mystical experience is that it resembles nothing of the world. It can be compared to nothing. But a man or woman who has the experience, as Ramakrishna has said, exudes a fragrance. We know he or she has reached to the higher dimensions. His behavior is balanced, moderate, wise, intelligent. He is sober.

Gene Kieffer: It is definitely not a vision that can be described?

Gopi Krishna: Higher consciousness is not a vision. It is a state of being. That is the difference. It is a state of being. I am *this*! I don't *see* anything external to myself. I see *myself* transformed in the higher consciousness. It is a vision of *myself*!

In a genuine mystical experience, there is clarity, lucidity. In fact, the clarity and the lucidity are a hundred times more powerful than in normal consciousness. It is not like a dream or a drug experience. You should read the original statements of the real mystics. What most people read are only the versions of modern writers, who can never understand the experience. In every genuine mystical experience, the individual is more clear and more lucid in his mind than he was in his normal state of consciousness. There is no transition. When you go from normal consciousness to sleep, there is a transition. You forget what you were. The same is true in the case of drugs. You have a transition. You were a normal person, but now you have different vision of lights, of sounds, or of bizarre experiences. But it is not like this in the case of mystical experience. It is just as though you walk straight into another world, of course, insensitive to this world for the moment, but with your inner faculties all completely alert.

Gene Kieffer: You have said that this experience can lead to the state of genius.

Gopi Krishna: It could be. I will give you some examples. Take the case of the greatest musicians. They have an awareness of those subtle melodies and notes which are not very easily perceptible to normal human beings. Great painters have a sense of colors and their harmony, a sense of symmetry, of natural grandeur which the common people miss. That means that they have become more sensitive to sound and to sight, which is a characteristic of higher consciousness.

Gene Kieffer: But in your case, you say you have undergone a complete change in a physiological sense, also.

Gopi Krishna: It took me years to research all those subtle changes in my perception. I have described that in my books. It didn't happen in one day. At first I only saw an expanded field of vision, and I also observed that whatever object I saw had a sort of white coat over it, like a white dust, like a chalk dust. Slowly this chalk dust was transformed into a silvery sheen. And now every color, every picture appears to me so fascinating that I would like to go on looking, at the sky for instance, for hours.

Gene Kieffer: But at the same time you say you also underwent an intellectual change and that your intellect is different now from what it had been.

Gopi Krishna: Yes, intellectual, mental, esthetic, moral— every transformation—and I am still being transformed. For instance, in my writing you can see a change. I think it will go on as long as I live. I feel mentally more alert and more active than I was at the age of 50, or 40. I feel more happy, more creative, with a greater zest for life. It has been a complete metamorphosis.

Gene Kieffer: You have described that you can sometimes discern the changes to your nervous system internally.

Gopi Krishna: I will offer my body to science. There is absolutely no doubt that there must be changes in my blood, also in my cerebrospinal fluid, tissues, in the nervous system above all.

Gene Kieffer: Can you observe what is going on internally?

Gopi Krishna: Yes. I now observe this nerve energy's flow, something that normal human beings cannot do. Because now this nerve energy, this psychic energy, this mental energy, like a powerful electric current, is self-luminous. It is shining. I can see it traversing my nerves, going into my brain, doing everything in my body.

Gene Kieffer: Do you live in this state 24 hours a day?

Gopi Krishna: Yes, 24 hours. There is no diminution, except in illness. But still, it is there, only then it is in a state of, I should say, disturbance. But most of the time my calmness, my inner happiness, continue. So long as the illness is there, however, I am not so alert. In fact, my illness starts first from the mind. I then become aware that the body will be indisposed, because I first detect changes in my mind.

Gene Kieffer: Could you speak more of illumination, since this is a state of consciousness on which so little has been written, especially in the past two or three decades.

Gopi Krishna: It is extremely difficult to talk about illumination. It has always been held that mystical experience is incommunicable. The descriptions given by the illuminati of ancient times are usually metaphorical or figurative. No one has attempted a clear description of this state, nor as far as I can see, is it possible to do so. If the vision of a savior is seen, it is bathed in light. If Christ, or Vishnu, or Krishna, or Muhammad, or any of the prophets is perceived, there is a glory surrounding the face and the figure.

Gene Kieffer: You have attempted to describe mystical experience in your books. Can you make such an attempt now?

Gopi Krishna: I shall try to convey a dim picture of what is perceived in the genuine mystical state. In normal consciousness, we see the world surrounding us on every side. We see the sky, the earth, the rivers, the mountains, the crowds, things like that. And while observing all this, we find ourselves to be observers, a puny pool of consciousness, a small unit of awareness which is experiencing all these things at any given moment. In the mystical experience, however, the roles are reversed. What we now perceive is the knower in us spread everywhere. We experience that the dominating entity is our soul, the knower. The world is reduced to the secondary position of a phantom.

In every case of mystical experience, whether a divine personality, a void, or an abstract of consciousness is perceived, the impression always is that one is in the presence of a universal entity, a sovereign, a master. We are in the presence of an overlord which dominates everything.

The illuminated mind is, in *actual fact, illuminated.* Whoever has given a description of mystical experience has invariably mentioned light, luminosity, luster, radiance or something to show that the vision has a brilliance and splendor associated with it.

Every mystic considered the vision that was unfolded before him as the vision of God or a Divine Being. This is because in the mystical state consciousness assumes a majesty, grandeur and all-pervasiveness, which is amazing. It is something beyond our thought in the normal waking state.

Gene Kieffer: This may be covering the same ground over and over again, but there can hardly be any question more in need of a direct answer than this one concerning the fake and real religious experience. Are there any methods that one can apply in getting to the bottom of this question?

Gopi Krishna: One method is to ask the subject of the experience to describe it. In the mystical literature of the world, every great mystic more or less described his own experience in his own original language. It is not borrowed from the language of others.

Gene Kieffer: How can you claim that you have experienced mystical consciousness? What new knowledge are you giving to the world?

Gopi Krishna: Frankly speaking, I do not claim that I am giving some new knowledge to the world. But my experience has taught me certain facts and granted me new insights into mystical experience, which were not known before and which no one has given during recent times. I say, on the basis of my experience that the human brain is still in a state of organic evolution. I say this in contradiction of the views held by most leading biologists at this moment. I say that this biological evolution is carrying all the race towards a higher state of consciousness, the same state possessed by the great prophets, like Buddha and Christ, of olden days. I further say that all the prophets and sages of mankind have been specimens of the future man to come, born before their time, and that the wisdom they have given is natural to the higher dimensions of consciousness.

There is a mechanism in the human body—psychophysiological mechanism, known as kundalini, which is the source from which inspiration, revelation and psychic gifts originate. Every person who is a psychic, a genius, or an enlightened sage, has an awakened kundalini to a greater or lesser extent.

Gene Kieffer: You have written that this mechanism is also behind certain intractable disorders of the mind like schizophrenia, or manic-depressive psychosis.

Gopi Krishna: Yes, definitely, and once this mechanism is known and investigated by scientists, millions of people will be benefitted by what I say. The cure of insanity will then become much easier than it is now. I am sure that if scientists were to give up all prejudice and prepossession and turn their attention to mystical experience, making experiments on what I am saying, they would confirm every word that I have written in my books. This is all in the fruit of the higher state of consciousness to which I have attained. There is no other man, to my knowledge, who has revealed these facts about the evolutionary mechanism, kundalini, or higher consciousness. Most of them are repeating what is already contained in the ancient books in India and other places.

Gene Kieffer: One last question. You seem to insist that the most effective way to counter the overhanging threat of a nuclear war is through the widespread dissemination of this kind of knowledge. Why?

Gopi Krishna: Because humanity as a whole has lost faith in a divine plan or source of life. The intelligentsia is mostly skeptical, too. The reason for this is that no serious effort has ever been made to investigate the claims of religion. An investigation into kundalini would show that human evolution is planned, that it does not happen at random or by the agency of natural selection alone.

Gene Kieffer: You say that evolution leads to a predetermined target?

Gopi Krishna: Definitely. The arousal of kundalini leads to certain biological changes in the system and ultimately to the manifestation of a higher consciousness, which we call mystical consciousness or enlightenment. Psychology summarily rejects enlightenment as something divine and instead ascribes it to the subconscious.

How can we bring conviction to the world that there is a divine ruler of the universe, that human life is programmed, that there is a target for human beings to achieve, and, above all, that human life has a purpose and a plan?

The answer is by doing research on kundalini. Once this is established—that this divine force works in a predetermined direction, that there is already a provision in the human body for the manifestation of this force—science will have to change its direction. It will then become obvious that evolution is planned, that there must be a super-intelligence ruling the universe.

Gene Kieffer: Still, how would this help to avert a nuclear war?

Gopi Krishna: Once human beings are convinced that there is an intelligence behind the universe, that their life is planned and has a purpose, and that by following a certain disciplined way of life—by meditation, prayer, worship or by altruistic deeds—they can attain the lofty states of sovereignty, they would then be able to curtail their passions, ambitions and desires. The divine incentive offered would be much greater than what they could ever achieve if they gained wealth, power, position and rulership.

When this path is opened and confirmed by science, people will discipline themselves. The leaders—the scholars and scientists—will all try to reach the same state of transcendence, which is the target of human evolution. That would provide a healthy exercise for their intellects and for their daily effort so that better government, a more catholic science, and a broader religion will take the place of the present ways of government, the present science, and the present churches. When this happens, war will automatically be eliminated.

ON THE SOVEREIGNTY
OF MYSTICAL EXPERIENCE

The following interview was compiled from the files of the Kundalini Research Foundation Ltd., by its director, Gene Kieffer. It is a combination of several interviews and originally appeared in *Science of Mind* magazine, October 1982.

Gene Kieffer: For more than a decade, you have been writing books on consciousness, evolution, and mystical experience. But despite the persuasiveness of your viewpoints, they have tended not to be accepted by conventional thinkers. Do you know why this has been so?

Gopi Krishna: The main problem is that there is still a great deal of confusion about the phenomenon known as mystical ecstasy. The general impression is that it is just an altered state of awareness, comparable to the states brought about by intoxicants, mind-altering drugs, hypnosis, biofeedback, hypnogogic conditions, and the like. Even an authority like William James was in error in the comparison he made between mystical ecstasy and the states induced by wine and nitrous oxide.

Gene Kieffer: Why has this confusion occurred?

Gopi Krishna: Because the transcendental and transhuman nature of mystical experience is still an uncharted province for scholars. There is a wide gulf between scholarship and mystical vision. The staggering nature of this vision and the revolution it brings about in the life and thinking of one who is blessed with it—and the light it throws on the problems of existence—are all beyond the power of intellect to grasp.

Gene Kieffer: In what way is it beyond the power of intellect?

Gopi Krishna: Intellectual study is like the data gathered by a dreamer in a dream world where he dwells for a while. The mystical vision is like the awareness gained when one is awake. I must make this clear with all the emphasis at my command and in full conformity to what has been as emphatically stated by mystics of the past— that the objective world disappears, like a phantom, in the illuminating blaze of mystical consciousness. The reality which is unveiled in the duration of the experience is beyond the grasp of the intellect and the power of language to describe.

Gene Kieffer: Do you think that contemporary scientists and intellectuals can even be expected to understand this reality, considering the nature of their training and experience?

Gopi Krishna: Not any more than the intellectual prodigies of the past, such as Shakespeare or Bacon, might have been expected to understand the awful force of the atom. Most present-day intellectuals believe they are almost at the frontiers of knowledge, but they have no inkling that the real quest of man has yet to begin. All the knowledge and experience they have gained, all the discoveries they have made, and all the inventions wrought so far, have been just preparation for the next step in man's progress, which is the exploration of his own mind to answer the riddle of his being.

Gene Kieffer: But scientists, in general, do not acknowledge the need to probe this riddle.

Gopi Krishna: Exactly. The human intellect, proud of its knowledge, is seldom ready to believe that there are worlds and regions beyond its reach.

Gene Kieffer: Isn't contemporary scientific research on consciousness making some progress?

Gopi Krishna: Research on consciousness, as it is being carried out today, is like an investigation done by a dreamer into the mental condition of the personalities in his dream. For one who lacks awareness about himself, however erudite he might be, the issue will always arise, who will do the research—and on what? How can one who does not understand himself or the real nature of his own mind, study the mind of another?

Gene Kieffer: So investigators must acknowledge that the "ordinary" state of awareness experienced by most people is extremely limited.

Gopi Krishna: Yes, exactly. According to Indian masters, who have contributed most to the study of the mind, *turiya*, or the fourth state of consciousness experienced in the mystical trance, is the real state of human awareness. The other three below it—namely, deep sleep, dreaming, and the normal wakeful state—are delusive. The "normal" state lends substance to a false appearance which hides the true reality.

Gene Kieffer: Then research on consciousness should begin with a study of one's own way of perceiving reality.

Gopi Krishna: Yes. This is what the ancient sages and seers did in their quest for enlightenment. During recent times, however, there has been hardly any new addition to the brilliant galaxy of enlightened prophets and sages of the past, because there has been no significant achievement in the search for self-understanding. This is also why there has been no fresh accumulation of knowledge of the transcendental state or any noteworthy addition to the information contained in the scriptures of mankind. The human race has become extravagantly rich in the knowledge of the world and physical comforts, but even poorer than before in the surpassing treasures of the mind. The erudite do not even suspect that "reason," on which *Homo sapiens* prides itself, is a kind of bondage. Used properly, the rational faculty is a most precious, indispensable instrument, but it has definite limitations.

Gene Kieffer: What is necessary if human beings are to undertake research on consciousness or a study of the mind?

Gopi Krishna: It is necessary, at least, to have some knowledge of the varied ways in which the phenomenon of consciousness is manifested. We know some of the extraordinary forms the mind can take, but they are unexplained by science. Most people with traditional education are all at sea in explaining psychic phenomena: they are still in conflict and confusion about dreams; they're in doubt and in a dilemma about the causes of insanity, in bewilderment about exceptional talent, and entirely in the dark about the nature and reality of mystical experience. What area of consciousness, therefore, can they profitably explore?

Gene Kieffer: But they believe they are making progress.

Gopi Krishna: I know. But still, whatever might be the field of scientific inquiry, it can never reveal consciousness in a state of freedom. It will always be bound by the walls of the sensory world and chains forged by the rational sense. The searching self will always remain a firefly, flitting from point to point in the darkness of infinity, as the human mind always does, never gathering the brilliance of a powerful lamp to dispel the shadows that surround it. This is the tragedy of the intellect. It is content with only a feeble glimmer of light that guides its steps a few paces. It can never imagine a splendor which lights a whole area at once.

Gene Kieffer: So you don't think science has made any really significant strides in the territory of consciousness or is any nearer to unraveling the mystery of the mind?

Gopi Krishna: Ask yourself. Has the study of insanity, high talent, sleep, hypnosis, or psychic phenomena carried out during the last century brought us any nearer to the end of our quest or made us any wiser about the riddle of existence? When our study of the outer world during the same period has yielded such a rich harvest in transforming the life of human beings, why do we find the doors tightly shut in our exploration of the inner realm?

Gene Kieffer: This is the crux of the problem. We know the physical world, but not the spiritual. What understanding do you offer us?

Gopi Krishna: As one who has been granted a brief glimpse into this profound mystery, I can say with confidence that no amount of objective study of consciousness undertaken over the next hundreds of years with the methods employed at present would lead the learned any nearer to the solution of this enigma. On the contrary, hundreds of volumes of new but confusing data would result, and the investigation would only make the situation more bewildering than before.

Gene Kieffer: Why?

Gopi Krishna: Because objective imagination, as it has been traditionally carried out, cannot bring more understanding to this phenomenon. Consciousness research demands a new approach. Evolving man must now shift his attention from the outer to the inner world, make *himself* the laboratory, and reverently approach the spirit within to instruct him in the rudiments of this science.

Gene Kieffer: There seems to be an instinctive longing in many people to return to nature, for instance, and to break away from today's highly complex, hectic life. Isn't all this an indication of a coming revolution in thinking?

Gopi Krishna: Yes. The stage is being set for this radical change in the direction of human effort from the outer to the inner world. The learned are usually not able to read the signs because the future is entirely shut from their view, and they have no idea that the revolution in the outer life of mankind will be a complement to the evolutionary change which has occurred within.

Gene Kieffer: Will you describe the essence of this inner evolutionary change?

Gopi Krishna: It has to do with the existence of a potential in the brain that can transform human life and bestow undreamed of intellectual, supersensory, and artistic gifts on individuals in a manner beyond imagination at present.

Gene Kieffer: Intellectuals should be able to grasp that, but you say most of them have no grounding in mysticism, so they continue to apply the same methods of analysis and criticism to which they are accustomed in other branches of knowledge.

Gopi Krishna: It is a sad commentary on the academic life of our time that a subject treated with respectful attention and reverential regard by the greatest intellectuals of the past, including such giants as Plato and Newton, should appear so trivial and unimportant to our intellectuals that they deem it beyond their dignity to study it with real care and attention.

Gene Kieffer: Do you believe your ideas can be communicated in the language of modern psychology?

Gopi Krishna: Probably not. Modern psychology is bristling with internal conflicts and controversies, and also the pulls and pressures from individual authorities each contradicting the other. How can a study based on a mistaken conception of mind, with excessive emphasis on the beast and chilling silence over the God in man, provide a suitable vehicle for explaining the profundities of consciousness or its triumphant march from the sub-human to the superhuman plane?

Gene Kieffer: Then what is the solution?

Gopi Krishna: The moment it is demonstrated that the human brain is still in a state of organic evolution in a *pre-planned direction,* not only the current theory of evolution but also psychological systems which are based primarily on the animal origin of mind rather than on its infinitely intelligent cosmic character, will come toppling to the earth.

How can we reconcile the divine nature of consciousness with some of the explanations offered by psychologists? The universe is a vast amphitheater, and the dramas enacted by consciousness on this stage from one end to the other, infinitely varied in plot and action, are yet closely interwoven and interconnected in a manner far beyond the grasp of the human intellect. Humanity will have to rise to dizzy heights of evolution before it can begin to comprehend the bewildering play of life. From Euclidean space we have come to the curved space of relativity, but there are already indications to show that is not the end. Who knows what new surprises are in store for astrophysicists in the years to come? It is likewise a fallacy to suppose that we have come to the end of the knowledge of mind.

Gene Kieffer: Don't you claim to be in possession of extraordinary knowledge?

Gopi Krishna: I have never laid any claim to a higher position than the one I possess. In fact, I have emphatically tried my utmost to make it clear that mystical experience does not represent a vision of God, but only a passage into a new dimension of consciousness which involves an aspect of glory and sovereignty not present at the human plane. I have also asserted repeatedly that, in all other aspects, I belong to the class of normal human beings, with the frailties and vanities common to human nature. Nowhere in my writings have I made any claim to sainthood or nearness to God or to a superhuman stature, though that is often done by God-men simply to point out the gulf that exists between them and the normal run of human beings.

Gene Kieffer: But you do claim to reside in the transcendental state of consciousness, do you not?

Gopi Krishna: Yes, but I endeavor to be clear that the transcendental state of consciousness, experienced as ecstasy by prophets and mystics throughout the past, does not signify a special favor from an anthropomorphic deity. It is only a more extended dimension of the perceptual faculty toward which mankind is evolving irresistibly, through the operation of an evolutionary, biological mechanism in the body. This mechanism has been designated as *kundalini* by the sages of India in the past.

Gene Kieffer: While this awareness of kundalini has existed for many years, you discuss it in the language of reason, without relying on supernatural mythical explanations.

Gopi Krishna: Yes. Kundalini is a monumental discovery which was made by the illuminati of India, and I am only presenting that knowledge in terms understandable to modern science. I have also repeatedly said that the interpretations I am placing on this phenomenon would be beyond my own capacity except for a strange dispensation of fate—the vast process of nature, guided by divine intelligence beyond my comprehension—by which I became the participant in an experience that unfolded the secret to me.

What I am trying to emphasize in all my work is that we have our existence in *two worlds*—the world of matter and the world of mind. As the result of an inquiry that has persisted through a prodigious span of time—ever since the dawn of reason—we have come into possession of a huge amount of knowledge of the material world, which is available for study by any one of us. But the study of the world of spirit requires entry into a new plane of consciousness and a supersensory channel of cognition, both of which are slowly coming into the possession of man through evolution. This is the purpose of the mystical trance or the transhuman states of consciousness exhibited by the prophets and the mystics of the world. They sang praises of the glory of God because the plane of being where they arrived *is* a plane of splendor, beauty, and transport, surpassing anything conceivable by a normal mind.

Gene Kieffer: But even so, if I understand you correctly, it is a plane just a little higher than that of normal human beings.

Gopi Krishna: You are perfectly correct. Those men and women who arrogate to themselves an extraordinary stature or position of authority by claiming to be unique incarnations of, or surrogates for the divine, must have a poor opinion about the staggering dimensions of the universe or the inconceivable proportions of its almighty creator.

Gene Kieffer: Because the transhuman state simply represents an evolutionary advance beyond the normal state of consciousness?

Gopi Krishna: Yes. Contrary attitudes could be justified in the prophets, sages, and seers of the past, when the vision of man was bounded by the earth alone and they had no idea of what gigantic worlds lay beyond—that a countless host of colossal suns and planets dwells in space. But from a God-man of today, the statements of the kind which were made in the scriptures of the past should be an affront to the intelligence.

Gene Kieffer: What is your belief about the future of humankind?

Gopi Krishna: From my point of view, future luminaries of the race, adorned with transhuman consciousness, will still be occupied with exploring the mystery of creation. But they will do so on higher planes of being, which are now imperceptible to us—in the same way that we are presently occupied with the exploration of the material universe. Most present-day concepts about the mind, its behavior, urges and appetites, are mere capricious intellectual excursions into a territory which needs another channel of cognition to explore.

Gene Kieffer: How does this "other channel" of cognition compare with a direct perception of the fullness of God?

Gopi Krishna: You said yourself that this other channel involves a plane of being a little higher than that of normal human consciousness, which is perfectly correct. But it does not merit comparison or equality with the infinite majesty and splendor of God. It is a variation of almost the same kind as we observe when we rise in the scale of life from the lower species to the higher ones. It amuses me to find that people in general, including scholars, often elevate mystics and enlightened saints to the stature of gods who cease to be humans, belonging to a world of superhuman dimensions and possibilities where they can defy the laws of nature, change the fate of common men and women, or do whatever they please. This is a serious error which stands as an impediment to understanding the mystical trance and to placing this extraordinary state of mind on a rational footing.

Gene Kieffer: Do you welcome the efforts of scholars and psychologists who write, to the best of their knowledge and skill, about consciousness?

Gopi Krishna: Certainly. But in fairness to all, I must point out that except in the case of those who have experienced the transformation, no scholar, merely with the exercise of his intellect, however versatile and learned he might be, can fathom the mystery.

How does eternal consciousness come to be embodied and then rise, step by step, through eons of time, to the realization of its own sovereignty? This is a riddle so profound that it is hard even to gauge its proportions. I must also add that present-day ideas about psychology, which emanated from Freud and others, offer only short-range explanations. These explanations will be subject to radical change from time to time as more and more knowledge is gained by the illuminati of the future about the nature and working of the mind and the organ of its expression, the brain.

Gene Kieffer: Your opinion of modern psychology is rather unflattering.

Gopi Krishna: The eternal riddles have excited curiosity from the dawn of reason to this day, and still we have not found an answer that could solve them once and for all. This is also the case with the riddle of the mind. The human intellect often takes delight in providing explanations even for those phenomena which are beyond its probe, such as the existence of God and the origin of the universe, the nature of the soul, and life after death. We can compare the present views of most psychologists to the ideas of alchemists before the modern science of chemistry came into existence.

Gene Kieffer: And you propose an experiment which will modernize the knowledge of mind?

Gopi Krishna: I hope to divest mystical ecstasy of both ancient superstition and modern intellectual confusion by drawing attention to the biological factors responsible for it. This objectification of the phenomenon has never been attempted before and the learned world is still unaware of it, or, if aware, is very skeptical. That unawareness demonstrates the entirely unsuspected nature of the phenomenon. From my point of view, mystical ecstasy is a *human* experience, the outcome of an organic process at work in the brain which signifies the first beginning of transhuman capacities in man.

Gene Kieffer: Isn't your position basically identical to what most other authorities on consciousness have said?

Gopi Krishna: No. I do not say that the human mind is evolving toward an undefined summit as, for instance, Teilhard de Chardin and others have said. What I firmly assert is that human consciousness is evolving toward a *predetermined target*, which I have experienced, and that this target is the mystical or illuminated state attained by thousands of mystics and enlightened human beings in the past. I also suggest that the religious scriptures of mankind are a harvest of the revelations received from a higher intelligence in this state of exalted being. What I further affirm is that the human brain is evolving toward this state of transhuman perception through the activity of an organic mechanism named *kundalini* by the ancients, whose existence can be demonstrated with methods known to science.

Gene Kieffer: This is a monumental assertion, since science has been attempting to discover this organic mechanism for decades without any success whatsoever.

Gopi Krishna: Exactly! And from all I am saying it follows that my goal is to place the whole domain of religion and of mystical ecstasy on the footing of a regular science, demonstrable with empirical methods. But the laboratory for the demonstration has to be the human body itself.

Gene Kieffer: Your writings include a good deal about other mental phenomena in addition to mystical ecstasy. Could you elaborate on these?

Gopi Krishna: My whole philosophy can be summed up in a few words. Therefore, it is not necessary that my books be read and reread to arrive at the conclusions I have drawn from my experience. I claim that the commonly known abnormal and paranormal states of mind, such as retardation, neurosis, or insanity on the one hand, and exceptional talent or paranormal gifts on the other, all proceed from the working of the evolutionary mechanism—kundalini—and that, with advanced knowledge of this mechanism, the problems resulting from its malfunctioning can be cured or obviated, and the precious attributes which it evokes can be cultivated at will.

Gene Kieffer: This appears to be a new contribution to the knowledge of man.

Gopi Krishna: To the best of my understanding, no other philosopher or mystic of the past has given the same interpretation to mystical experience and presented a cut-and-dried formula. Please keep in mind that

I am not putting forward an intellectual dissertation based on mere erudition and logic. I am submitting a concrete proposal based on a personal study of the phenomenon for laboratory experiment to validate. If these conclusions are proven, they will be of colossal importance for the race.

Gene Kieffer: If this is the case, why haven't these disclosures been greeted with acclaim?

Gopi Krishna: Because the ideas expressed are new and original, and therefore need time to take root in the common mind. Also, they strongly militate against some of the current conceptions or misconceptions of both orthodox science and religion. How can the erudite, on either side, readily swallow the utterances of someone who says that matter is a mirage? Darwin was wrong, Freud was mistaken—consciousness is all.

That humanity is on its way to this awareness in the beatific state, that the great illuminati were not and could not be simply the special favorites of the almighty, and that mystical experience does not represent an encounter with God, but only a vision of the divinity in man—that is what I proclaim.

Gene Kieffer: Then what is needed is something like a new Manhattan Project, which would call together the world's finest minds to test your theory scientifically.

Gopi Krishna: Yes. Only by a deep study of this thesis can an unbiased intellect recognize that no other single interpretation synthesizes the diversity of religious experience and outlook, serves as a connecting link between religion and science, and brings science back from a lopsided, entirely materialistic view of the universe toward a more rational and comprehensive philosophy of creation—one in which matter and mind figure as the two aspects of one incomprehensible reality, dimly perceptible in another dimension of consciousness, of which religion is the still growing child.

The problem is that it is hard for an intellectual to accept the position that his territory ends at the very beginning of the mystical trance. And, characteristic of the intellect, it is seldom prepared to accept defeat and is often overconfident of its ability to know all that can be known. But the tittle-tattle of irrepressible mental gossip finally comes to an end when one is face-to-face with the unbelievable splendor of the mystical vision, hushed into silence at the awesome majesty of the reality which is unfolded there.

Epilogue:
Kundalini in the New Age

We have now taken a fairly comprehensive look at kundalini. Is it real? Or should stories about kundalini be relegated to the manic imaginings of a few deluded, hysterical individuals? Are the kundalini awakenings that Gopi Krishna, Krishnamurti, Dr. Motoyama, and I described genuine? Surely they are, and any inquiry that sets aside prejudices of religious belief or disbelief, or that goes beyond principles espoused by particular schools of psychology should be able to perceive here evidence of real, literal fact. The reports given in the kundalini narratives correspond so identically—the flames, the intense heat, the visions, the voices, the current rising up the spine, the transcendent moment of illumination—these correspondences alone testify to the authenticity of these accounts. Moreover, these descriptions are similar to those chronicled in the ancient texts of kundalini and throughout the history of the human race.

One can cite some of the Christian mystics, for example, like the 16th-century Carmelites, St. Theresa of Avila, or St. John of the Cross. Some of St. Theresa's experiences are very suggestive of kundalini: her severe headaches, the uncontrollable shivering during her altered states, or the convulsions powerful enough to

throw her involuntarily from her bed. There were levitating incidents too, whereby without the use of her
hands she would spring from her knees to land standing on her head (presumably supported by her hands);
and then there was, as she described it, her "flight of the
spirit . . . a movement of the soul . . . so swift it seems
the spirit is carried off, and at a fearful speed. . . ."[1]
Although such occurrences were welcome and seen as a
gift from God, she remarked that "great courage is necessary, for the favor is something frightening."[2] Her
confrere and occasional traveling companion, St. John of
the Cross, also reported kundalini-like experiences.
Mark these stanzas from the *Ascent of Mount Carmel* by
St. John:

> I went forth without being observed,
> My house being now at rest.
> In darkness and secure,
> By the secret ladder, disguised
> —oh, happy chance!—
>
> . . . . .
>
> . . . As I parted his locks;
> With his gentle hand he wounded my neck
> And caused all my senses to be suspended.[3]

St. John informs us that in the second stanza the phrase
"In darkness and secure" refers to the spiritual detachment of the soul as it leaves (I went forth), the body (My
house), and ascends to God. This is accomplished by
means of the "Divine ladder of faith, which attains and
penetrates even to the heights of God."[4] On this ladder,
"all the rungs and parts are secret and hidden from all
sense and understanding."[5]

This ladder and its secret and incomprehensible rungs penetrating to God appear to allude to the chakras of the cerebrospinal system and the ascent of kundalini to the Sahasrara, or Crown chakra. And in the bottom stanza one recognizes in the wound in the neck the acute pain and burning in the nape of Krishnamurti's neck or the lump on the back of my neck. Granted, St. John may not be referring to kundalini here and may be portraying a Christian theme, for instance, the idea of coming face to face with God. But these Christian metaphors do very strongly suggest the imagery of kundalini.

Evidence of kundalini has appeared in the writings, language, and artifacts of many cultures. It was known to the ancient Egyptians and Maya; it was known in China, Korea, Greece, and Tibet; it is known to the Sufis and to Native Americans; it is known in Africa as well. Lee Sannella, in *Kundalini — Psychosis or Transcendence?*[6] quotes from "Education for Transcendence: Lessons from the !Kung Zhu Twasi" by R. Katz[7] describing the practices of the !Kung people of the Kalahari Desert in Northwest Botswana, Africa, who dance for many hours to 'heat' up the *n/um* so that the *!kia* state can be attained. [Katz notes] that *n/um* is analogous to the kundalini state. "!Kia is the state of transcendence."[8] Here are two descriptions:

(1) Then n/um lifts you in your belly and lifts you in your back, and then you start to shiver. N/um makes you tremble; it's hot.... n/um enters every part of your body, right to the tip of your feet and even your hair.

(2) In your backbone you feel a pointed something, and it works its way up. Then the base of your spine is tingling, tingling, tingling, tin-

gling, tingling, tingling, tingling . . . and then it
makes your thoughts nothing in your head.[9]

The !kia is an intense emotional state. At its height, the
n/um master practices extraordinary activities such as
curing the sick, handling and walking on fire; a master
has X-ray vision and may see over great distances, but
does not even attempt such activities in his ordinary
state.[10]

Katz points out that "over half the tribe members
can attain this state and !kia seems to run in families."[11] It
is considered "painful, fearful, and unpredictable,"[12] and
guru/student relationships are formed to make sure that
"excessive fear does not prevent the occurrence of !kia."[13]

The !Kung people "seek !kia not only for their own
personal enrichment, but to help others. . . . An
extended !kia is not seen as a state of grace but as a mistake. !Kia is for entering the religious dimension,
receiving its nourishment, sharing it in healing, and
then to return and live this truth" with one's family and
neighbors.[14]

Let us continue then, by stating that kundalini has
always existed and that it is a biological process. Even
though the mental productions and manifestations are
extremely mystical, the underlying process is still biological and mechanical. Enough evidence exists to support
this viewpoint even though at present this phenomenon
has yet to be verified by science. This is, however, not a
major concern. There are many wonders of nature about
which science knows very little or nothing, but that
doesn't disprove their existence. Bacteria and its functions were only discovered in the last century and the
double helix of DNA is a comparatively recent discovery,
as was the discovery of vitamins. Kundalini will eventually have its day in the laboratory too.

More than anything else, kundalini is a healing and transformative process. The healing and transformation are both physiological and psychological, for kundalini thoroughly galvanizes the neurological pathways and opens up previously closed circuits of the brain and nervous system. The result is that pockets of guilt and rage are eliminated, the intelligence is advanced, and the spirit is reenergized. Gopi Krishna wrote, "by using a more potent *prana* and the precious substances, present in the reproductive secretions, [kundalini] starts an amazing process of remodeling designed to form a supersensory compartment in the brain—the ultimate object of the evolutionary impulse still active in man."[15] Here is Gopi Krishna on healing:

> For a long time I could not understand what hidden purpose was being served by the unremitting flow of the new-born nervous radiation and what changes were being wrought in the organs and nerves and in the structure of the brain. . . . Immediately after the crisis, however, I noticed a marked change in my digestive and eliminatory functions. . . . It appeared as if I were undergoing a process of purgation, of internal purification of the organs and nerves, and that my digestive apparatus was being toned to a higher pitch of efficiency.[16]

Reflecting on my own experience, I, too, thought of healing and transformation. I began to feel, at last, a sense of peace and well-being, and it struck me that I was undergoing some sort of healing process, that by going through the storms I was becoming divested of traumatic knots that had built up over the course of my life.[17] Dr. Motoyama and Krishnamurti also reported continuing

202 • Darrel Irving

and long-term processes of experiences of transformation and healing.

Gopi Krishna called kundalini the key to the evolutionary mechanism. He contended that those who undergo the kundalini process are elevated to a new plane of consciousness and that not only genius, but talent and illumination as well, are attributable to kundalini. Gopi Krishna says, "The twin products of an active kundalini, namely the illuminati and the men and women of genius and talent, have been the two main classes of human beings responsible for every advance made by mankind so far."[18] Transformation does not, however, always reach these heights. There may be varying degrees of transformation. Gene Kieffer, in *The Secret of Kundalini*, points out that kundalini can "awaken and ascend into the brain just for an instant, at greatly reduced potency, and then return again to the base of the spine, leaving the person overcome with awe. In that brief moment, his whole life can change completely. New circuits, albeit limited in scope and complexity, will have been etched into his brain. If Kundalini does not withdraw but continues to circulate in the organism, then that same person becomes a sage, a rishi and a seer, or in other words, a prophet who is able to discern the future.[19]

Kieffer's description of a brief awakening is reminiscent of Dr. Richard Maurice Bucke. Dr. Bucke, who in 1900 published *Cosmic Consciousness*, one of the classic texts on mystical experience, and which examines the experience of enlightenment from a Western perspective, describes just how powerful that one brief instant can be. Here is his own personal account. He writes of himself in the third person.

It was in the early spring at the beginning of his thirty-sixth year. He and two friends had spent the evening reading Wordsworth, Shelley, Keats, Browning, and especially Whitman. They parted at midnight, and he had a long drive in a hansom (it was in an English city). His mind deeply under the influence of the ideas, images and emotions called up by the reading and talk of the evening, was calm and peaceful. He was in a state of quiet, almost passive enjoyment. All at once, without warning of any kind, he found himself wrapped around as it were by a flame colored cloud. For an instant he thought of fire, some sudden conflagration in the great city, the next he knew that the light was within himself. Directly afterwards came upon him a sense of exultation, of immense joyousness accompanied or immediately followed by an intellectual illumination quite impossible to describe. Into his brain streamed one momentary lightning-flash of the Brahmic Splendor which has ever since lightened his life; upon his heart fell one drop of Brahmic Bliss, leaving thenceforward for always an after taste of heaven. Among other things he did not come to believe, he saw and knew that the Cosmos is not dead matter but a living Presence, that the soul of man is immortal, that the universe is so built and ordered that without any peradventure all things work together for the good of each and all, that the foundation principle of the world is what we call love and that the happiness of every one is in the long run absolutely certain. He claims that he learned more within the few seconds during which the illumination lasted than in previous months or even years of study, and that he learned much that no study could ever have taught.

204 • Darrel Irving

The illumination itself continued not more than a few moments, but its effects proved ineffaceable; it was impossible for him ever to forget what he at that time saw and knew, neither did he, or could he, ever doubt the truth of what was then presented to his mind. There was no return that night or at any other time of the experience.[20]

Kieffer and Bucke have each pointed out that a person in whom kundalini awakens even momentarily is permanently changed. I, too, feel that I have never again been the same even though the entire kundalini process lasted less than twelve hours.

Partial awakenings of kundalini, in which the kundalini does not rise all the way to the brain, but goes to another center such as the heart or throat center, are also common. This kind of activation is also dramatic, and the process is also one of transformation. Dr. Motoyama, for example, reported extremely mystical and transcendental states in connection with all the chakras.

The consummate moment of kundalini awakening, though, is always marked by the rise of kundalini up the sushumna to or through the top of the head. This was described by Gopi Krishna as a zigzagging silvery streak that poured an "effulgent, cascading shower of brilliant vital energy"[21] into his brain; by Dr. Motoyama as his spiritual self gradually rising higher to leave his body through the top of his head;[22] by me as a swift, whirling, gyroscoping rush of energy up my spine and right out through the top of my head;[23] and now by Bucke as a momentary lightning flash of Brahmic Splendor streaming into his brain.[24]

Interestingly, Krishnamurti's description in which "the bally thing" ran up his spine to meet as a flame between his eyebrows could be construed as depicting the kundalini rising only to the Ajna chakra. Here then, is further confirmation of the illuminating power of chakras other than the Sahasrara. Beyond this, it is curious that this was the last account of kundalini reported by Krishnamurti. But considering his forgetfulness, his penchant for secrecy in private matters, and his distaste for the occult, it is understandable that he did not provide a record of later kundalini activity. It seems likely, nevertheless, that kundalini did continue its illuminating activity in his mind and body. He continued throughout his life to have mystical and transcendent experiences, for instance, when he told of reaching the source of all energy at the age of 84.[25] This description could only have been reported by someone who had undergone a profound transformation of consciousness.

In *Cosmic Consciousness,* Bucke's archetype is Walt Whitman, whom Bucke knew personally and described as "the best, most perfect, example the world has so far had of the Cosmic Sense."[26] And it is true that Walt Whitman was among the most sublime and exalted of human beings Bucke's accolade notwithstanding, in "Song of Myself," in the stanzas where Whitman tells of his awakening to higher consciousness, and I believe this is a description of the activation of kundalini; here too, there is no mention of the Sahasrara. Thus, on this occasion, at least, although illumined, Whitman may not have reached the highest level in terms of Chakra activation.

Many will undoubtedly object that these particular stanzas of "Song of Myself" are so sexually explicit they could not possibly refer to mystical experience. There are reasons, however, to consider them as just that, as symbolic descriptions of cosmic awakening. Bucke, who was, in fact, a member of Whitman's inner circle and about whom Whitman wrote, "Dr. Bucke is about the only one that thoroughly radiates and depicts and describes in a way I think thoroughly delineates me,"[27] was in a position to learn directly from Whitman his intended meaning in these stanzas. And Bucke does not even consider the sexual implications of these stanzas in his analysis. On the contrary, Bucke states that these stanzas are describing a new faculty, a new sense which came upon Whitman in June 1853 or 1854 when he was 34 or 35. In his commentary on this poem Bucke writes, "The illumination (or whatever it was) came to him or upon him one June morning, and took . . . absolute possession of him. . . . Henceforth, he says, his life received its inspiration from the newcomer, the new self, whose tongue, as he expresses it, was plunged to his bare-stripped heart."[28]

In the context of this illumination, then, here are those stanzas from "Song of Myself." They may signify more than a passionate tryst on a summer's day; rather they may be depicting Whitman's moment of union with the divine.

> I mind how once we lay such a transparent summer
>   morning,
> How you settled your head athwart my hips and
>   gently turn'd over upon me,
> And parted the shirt from my bosom-bone, and
>   plunged your tongue to my bare-stript heart,
> And reach'd till you felt my beard, and reach'd till
>   you felt my feet.
>
> Swiftly arose and spread around me the peace and
>   knowledge that pass all the argument of the
>   earth,
> And I know that the hand of God is the promise of
>   my own,
> And I know that the spirit of God is the brother of
>   my own,

And that all the men ever born are also my brothers,
and the women my sisters and lovers,
And that a kelson of the creation is love. . . .[29]

Now consider that these stanzas may be an ode to kundalini and its rising to the Anahata, or Heart chakra. For it seems entirely possible that Whitman intended the following symbolism:

(1) The speaker's hips are analogous to the Muladhara chakra at the base of the spine;

(2) "Settled your head . . . gently turn'd over upon me" describes the first stirrings of the kundalini energy;

(3) The tongue represents the kundalini rising to the bare-stript heart, the now-opened Anahata chakra;

(4) The kundalini continues up through the beard and down to the feet as it courses through the entire body.

The lines from these two stanzas are assuredly as dramatic a depiction of illumination as will be found anywhere. Seen in the context of kundalini, it is understandable why Whitman would have chosen sexual metaphors to express the experience. And, if I have interpreted the stanzas correctly, then as I have stated, there is no reference to the Sahasrara. The important point here is that in all instances, whether kundalini has been activated to the navel or to the crown center, the result in every case is one of remarkable transformation. Kundalini *is* the evolutionary mechanism in the human being.

Legitimately it could be asked, why, if kundalini is the evolutionary mechanism, is it so painful, so fraught with peril? But, as we have seen, there can be benign awakenings, too. (See Gopi Krishna's commentary in chapter 8.) In *The Secret of Kundalini,* Gene Kieffer describes a woman in Poughkeepsie, New York, in whom the kundalini process has been tranquil over a fifteen-year period. The process began spontaneously and gently, and as a result of the kundalini she has become a painter and poet. She remains amazed and surprised by the occurrences in her interior. "Wherever she looks whether within or without, her ever-expanding world is filled with wonders and entrancing light."[30] In addition to Kieffer's account, there are surely innumerable peaceful awakenings that are unreported.

That there are so few reports of kundalini arousal may be reason to conjecture that a deterioration of the kundalini centers occurs during childhood, caused by trauma engendered in early childhood training and conditioning. Children are extremely sensitive, and the neurological centers and pathways in which kundalini becomes active are still developing at this stage. If the childhood upbringing is too severe, the kundalini mechanism may virtually shut down, causing these centers and pathways to atrophy.

By the time children have passed from puberty into adulthood, their entire bodies—their hormones, glands, bones, and muscles—every part of them has undergone a dramatic, physiological change. But there is no sign of a corresponding development in the kundalini plexus, as indicated by the dearth of instances of kundalini arousal throughout the world. This suggests the possibility that in most individuals the kundalini plexus has become stunted, that the neurological pathways have not developed and are "covered with cobwebs" from all those years of disuse. If this proves to be true, then it follows that when kundalini finally is activated, either spontaneously or through various practices, the current would be too great for the undeveloped neurological conduits and outlets through which it courses. The result would be a mental breakdown—actually a physiological breakdown—while the kundalini undertakes the task of repairing and reopening the neurological system to accommodate the heightened kundalini energy.

How can society assist individuals in whom this kundalini suddenly has become operative? First, the healing and transformative aspects of kundalini must not be underestimated. This process, which until now has been viewed by psychiatry as mental disorder, as destructive, as an aberration to be responded to with institutionalization, antipsychotic drugs, and therapies designed to restore patients to their former states of mind, must be reevaluated and seen for what it is—a chance for real healing, for actual transformation—a process that no matter how painful, needs to be approached with unshakeable faith that nature knows best, and that the mechanisms of the body have been designed to be ultimately benevolent.

Special housing and treatment centers need to be constructed for all people in whom kundalini has become active, such as (1) individuals who have heretofore remained outside the arena of orthodox psychological treatment, for instance, yogis or people in whom kundalini has spontaneously awakened and who are struggling through the process in their own homes; and (2) individuals who have become delusional or who have been diagnosed as schizophrenic and are now undergoing orthodox psychiatric treatment. Gopi Krishna, for example, who would have belonged to the first group, did seek help and even thought of consulting a psychiatrist. He then thought better of it, realizing that his mental state was beyond the scope of traditional psychiatric methodology. Nevertheless, he would have welcomed competent help if it had been available.

A third category of kundalini-activated individuals would include those in whom the kundalini has awakened in a malignant manner, who are deranged, hostile, delusional, and dangerous. They too, require housing and treatment. The approach toward this group would differ, obviously, for first and foremost the civil rights of their neighbors must be protected. But the end purpose should be the elimination of the malignancy, not punishment. The outcome of a malignant kundalini can be quite positive if the kundalini is given the opportunity to run its course. For the storms and fires of kundalini have the power to transform, to burn away the pent-up rage that drives such persons to violence. This violent group, in particular, should be of primary concern for obvious reasons. If these individuals can be restored to health, the whole of society will thereby be elevated to a new plateau of well-being.

Ultimately, of course, yogis, schizophrenics, manic-depressives, lunatics, and delusional psychopaths alike, should all be rediagnosed as "kundalini-activated" patients and provided refuge from the storms their symptoms engender. All of these people require a safe environment where they can be nurtured through the ravaging fires of kundalini. The goal of such care would be to guide these individuals toward the altered, para-normal, and transcendent states of mind to which the kundalini process naturally evolves. No one would deny that the kundalini process can be exceedingly painful. But if allowed to progress to healing, the results can be extraordinary. To this end, an entirely new discipline of medical care, in which nurses and physicians are knowledgeable about kundalini, is imperative.

Kundalini is a dynamic and volatile process, and it cannot be stressed strongly enough that people undergoing this process need special care. The great Indian sage Ramakrishna used to go off into samadhi—in his case his body frequently went into a dead faint without warning—often while he was standing. This was no great problem, for Ramakrishna had many disciples all too happy to take care of his personal requirements as he passed in and out of altered states of consciousness.

But most people with an awakened kundalini do not have a host of disciples to look after them as Ramakrishna did. Many have neither friends nor family. A friend of mine has gone through twenty years as a diagnosed schizophrenic without the kind of support we are talking about here. Karen, as I will call her, first felt the onset of her symptoms while walking across campus at Columbia University where she had been a student. She was walking from the east side of the campus to the west side, and by the time she had walked across she was hallucinating, in a state of mental confusion, in the midst of what psychiatrists would call a full-blown psychotic episode. To this day she does not know what caused this. Karen wonders if someone slipped her a tab of LSD without her knowledge. But there are precipitating factors in her background that might predispose her to such experiences, including sexual abuse as a child and a history of "mental illness" in her family. My own view of this is that her predisposition is toward kundalini, not mental illness. Karen has been in and out of mental wards ever since her campus walk and goes through life sedated. Originally she did not request hospitalization; it was forced upon her by her parents who could not cope with the intensity of her so-called madness. As she describes it, "My God, it was incredible, I was literally levitating in the living room." It is not clear to me how much of Karen's "madness" her parents witnessed, but at a certain point they had seen enough; they called the caretakers in the white coats.

Karen is extremely psychic and describes terrifying visits to the netherworlds, but she also tells of an illuminating side to her inner world. Her reality-testing capacity has remained intact these entire twenty years; she has never been delusional, and she has always been very clear about what has happened to her and about who she is. About the whole experience, and especially with regard to kundalini, with which she is familiar, she says, "It's too much, I wouldn't want to go through it again. Kundalini? I don't know—maybe the illuminating parts of it, when I am old. Yes, it should be for older people."

Karen was hospitalized against her will and diagnosed as schizophrenic. Later on, for she had to get herself functioning somehow, she voluntarily entered an out-patient program at a hospital in New York City. Thus one could say that hospitalization was predestined for Karen—there was no other help available. She now takes antipsychotic drugs and is grateful for the suppression of her symptoms, though she detests the excess weight and the vagueness around the edges that go with the drugs. There are still areas of this experience that are seductive to her, but she will never allow herself to be drawn back over that edge if she can help it—the pain was simply too great.

People like Karen should never be forced into a mental institution, where they will be stigmatized as schizophrenic, numbed and endangered with antipsychotic drugs, and where the hope of a bright future is an unknown prognosis. Society owes itself and Karen much more. For if Karen can be retrieved and nurtured to the evolutionary consciousness envisioned by Gopi Krishna and to which her own kundalini could carry her if she were given a nurturing environment, then she and others like her are the promise and guiding light of the future.

Many people believe the human race is now entering a new era, the Aquarian age. This may be seen in the call for freedom ringing throughout the world, from the gathering strength of the Gay Rights movement to the momentum building in the Women's Liberation movement, from the demands for ecological reform to concern for the impoverished and homeless, and from a summons to all countries to join under one flag, a banner of peace uniting the nations of the earth, to the growing realization that racism is the issue of this decade and all those to come—for if we cannot recognize our common brotherhood, our common sisterhood, then our civilization will continue its plunge downward.

With such solemn concerns fanning across the planet, serious consideration, too, must be given to creating an environment in which kundalini can flower. Kundalini centers need to be established everywhere— kundalini schools and universities, kundalini medical facilities, kundalini laboratories, kundalini libraries, kundalini spiritual centers, kundalini social and political organizations. It is vitally important that kundalini become a prominent feature of contemporary life. The age we are leaving behind has been a dark and Godless one—we have become disconnected from God, we have become fearful and self-absorbed with little regard for the well-being of the less fortunate, with no driving sense to put things right so that all can share in the bounty of the planet. Kundalini is the energy that can propel the human race to direct knowledge of God, that is, to direct knowledge of the real self, to new spiritual values based upon that knowledge, to a new sense of freedom, to a humanitarianism that insists on fair and equitable distribution of the Earth's resources, and to a world society where privilege is not reserved for a sanctioned few, but is an entitlement belonging to everyone.

NOTES

Chapter 1

1. Gopi Krishna, *Kundalini, The Evolutionary Energy in Man* (Boston: Shambhala, 1967, 1970).

2. Sir John Woodroffe (Arthur Avalon), *The Serpent Power* (Madras, India: Ganesh & Co., Auromere, 1973).

3. Mary Scott, *Kundalini in the Physical World* (New York: Viking Penguin, 1990).

4. Ajit Mookerjee, *Kundalini: The Arousal of the Inner Energy* (Rochester, VT: Inner Traditions, 1983).

5. Jiddu Krishnamurti, *Thought Breeds Fear*, Talk given in London, March 16, 1969 (Ojai, CA: Krishnamurti Foundation of America); *Freedom from the Known* (San Francisco: HarperCollins, 1975); *Education and the Significance of Life* (San Francisco: HarperCollins, 1981); *Mind in Meditation*, Talk given in Bangalore, India, January 31, 1971 (Ojai, CA: Krishnamurti Foundation of America); *This Light in Oneself*, Talk given in Amsterdam, May 19, 1968 (Ojai, CA: Krishnamurti Foundation of America); *The Awakening of Intelligence* (New York: HarperCollins, 1987).

6. Mary Lutyens, *Krishnamurti: The Years of Awakening* (New York: Avon Books, 1975); *Krishnamurti: The Years of Fulfillment* (New York: Avon Books, 1975).

7. Pupul Jayakar, *Krishnamurti: A Biography* (San Francisco: HarperCollins, 1986).

Chapter 3

1. Gopi Krishna, *Kundalini: The Evolutionary Energy in Man* (Boston: Shambhala, 1967, 1970), p. 11.

2. Ibid., pp. 11–13.

3. Ibid., p. 17.

4. Ibid., p. 64.

5. Ibid., p. 66.

6. Ibid., p. 67.

7. Ibid.

8. Ibid., pp. 144–145.

9. Ibid., p. 146.

10. The Lord Maitreya was one of the unseen masters in the theosophical occult hierarchy who lives on the spiritual plane. Krishnamurti was taught that after various initiations he would be prepared one day to be the vehicle of Lord Maitreya's earthly reincarnation.

11. A theosophical concept: the part of the body that controls its instinctive and purely physical actions when the higher consciousness is withdrawn. It is at a low stage of evolution and needs guidance.

12. Mary Lutyens, *Krishnamurti: The Years of Awakening* (New York: Avon Books, 1975), p. 170.

13. *Krishnamurti: The Years of Awakening*, pp. 170–171.

14. According to theosophy, Master K. H. and the Lord Buddha, like the Lord Maitreya, are highly evolved spiritual beings inhabiting another spiritual plane.

15. *Krishnamurti: The Years of Awakening*, p. 171.

16. Ibid.

17. Ibid., pp. 178–179.

18. Ibid., pp. 179–180.

19. Ibid., p. 185.

20. The Brahman Gate is an opening in the crown of the head through which kundalini and prana may pass as they rise along the Sushumna channel.

21. Pupul Jayakar, *Krishnamurti: A Biography* (San Francisco: HarperCollins, 1986), p. 57.

22. *Krishnamurti: The Years of Awakening*, p. 202.

23. Archives of the Theosophical Society, Adyar, Madras.

24. *Krishnamurti: A Biography*, p. 128.

25. Mary Lutyens, *Krishnamurti: The Years of Fulfillment* (New York: Avon Books, 1975), p. 237.

27. Hiroshi Motoyama, *Theories of the Chakras: Bridge to Higher Consciousness* (Wheaton, IL: Theosophical Publishing House, 1981), pp. 240–241.

28. Ibid., p. 242.

29. Ibid.

30. Ibid., p. 247.

31. Ibid., p. 250.

32. Ibid.

33. Ibid.

34. Ibid.. pp. 250–251.

35. Ibid., pp. 251–252.

36. Ibid., p. 252.

37. Ibid., pp. 253–254.

38. Ibid., p. 256.

39. Joseph Campbell, *The Inner Reaches of Outer Space* (New York: HarperCollins, Perennial, 1988).p. 90.

Chapter 4

1. In occult thought, the chakras can connect to extrasensory bodies called the etheric, astral, mental, or causal bodies, existing in etheric, astral, mental, and causal realms.

2. Charles Webster Leadbeater, *The Chakras* (1927. Reprint: Wheaton, IL: Theosophical Publishing House, Quest Books, 1990).

3. Gopi Krishna, *Kundalini—The Secret of Yoga* (Darien, CT: The Kundalini Research Foundation, Ltd.; and Toronto: F.I.N.D. Research, 1972) p. 52.

4. Ibid., p. 53.

5. Ibid., p. 52.

6. Ibid., p. 56.

7. Gopi Krishna, *Kundalini, The Evolutionary Energy in Man* (Boston: Shambhala, 1967, 1970), p. 174.

8. *Kundalini—The Secret of Yoga*, p. 60.

9. Ibid.

10. Ibid., p. 59.
11. Ibid., p. 63.
12. Ibid., p. 64.
13. Hiroshi Motoyama, *Theories of the Chakras: Bridge to Higher Consciousness* (Wheaton, IL: Theosophical Publishing House, Quest, 1981), p. 241.
14. Ibid.
15. Ibid., p. 243.
16. Ibid., pp. 281–282.
17. Ibid., p. 238.
18. *The Chakras*, p. 4.
19. Ibid., p. 71.
20. Ibid., p. 54.
21. Ibid.
22. Ibid., p. 87.
23. Charles Webster Leadbeater, *Science of the Sacraments* (Wheaton, IL: Theosophical Publishing House, 1988).
24. This letter was previously cited on page 30. See Chapter 3, footnote 19.
25. Mary Lutyens, *Krishnamurti: The Years of Awakening* (New York: Avon Books, 1975), p. 185.
26. Ibid., p. 223.
27. *The Chakras*, p. 72.
28. Ibid., pp. 77–78.
29. *Theories of the Chakras*, p. 110.
30. *Kundalini—The Secret of Yoga*, p. 164.
31. Ibid., p. 163.
32. Ajit Mookerjee, *Kundalini: The Arousal of the Inner Energy* (Rochester, VT: Inner Traditions, 1983).

Chapter 5

1. See p. 20.
2. See p. 29.
3. See p. 49.
4. See p. 37.

5. Paul Schilder, *On Psychoses*, Lauretta Bender, ed. (New York: International Universities Press, 1975), p. 491.

6. Karl Jaspers, *General Psychopathology*, trans. J. Hoenig and M. W. Hamilton (Chicago: University of Chicago Press, 1963), p. 213.

7. Ibid.

8. Karl Leonard, trans. *The Classification of Endogenous Psychoses* (New York: Irvington Publishers, 1979), p. 306.

9. Ibid., p. 386.

10. Ibid., p. 325.

11. Ibid., p. 253.

12. *On Psychoses*, p. 489.

13. *General Psychopathology*, p. 467.

14. Ibid., p. 91.

15. Ibid., p. 92.

16. *The Classification of Endogenous Psychoses*, p. 314.

17. *General Psychopathology*, p. 146.

18. See p. 20.

19. See p. 20.

20. *Krishnamurti: The Years of Awakening*, p. 174.

21. Ibid., p. 178.

22. *The Classification of Endogenous Psychoses*, p. 84.

23. *General Psychopathology*, p. 62.

24. *On Psychoses*, p. 482.

25. *The Classification of Endogenous Psychoses*, p. 131.

26. Ibid., p. 310.

27. Ibid., p. 115.

28. Ibid., p. 111.

29. Ibid., p. 329.

30. Ibid., p. 89.

31. *General Psychopathology*, p. 87.

32. *The Classification of Endogenous Psychoses*, p. 325.

33. Ibid., p. 309.

34. Ibid., p. 317.

35. Ibid., p. 171.

36. *General Psychopathology*, p. 141.

37. *Theories of the Chakras*, p. 250.
38. Joanne Greenberg, *I Never Promised You a Rose Garden* (New York: Holt, Rinehart and Winston, 1964; NAL, 1989), p. 4.
39. See, pp. 49–50.
40. John Frosch, *The Psychotic Process* (New York: International Universities Press, 1983), p. 207.
41. Ibid., p. 208.
42. See p. 50.
43. *I Never Promised You a Rose Garden*, p. 90.
44. *The Classification of Endogenous Psychoses*, p. 386.
45. Ibid., p. 310.
46. *General Psychopathology*, p. 91.
47. *The Classification of Endogenous Psychoses*, p. 131.
48. Ibid., p. 112.
49. *On Psychoses*, p. 514.
50. Ibid., p. 486.
51. *The Classification of Endogenous Psychoses*, p. 68.
52. Ibid., pp. 69–70.
53. Ibid., pp. 180–181.
54. John White, ed. *Kundalini: Evolution & Enlightenment* (New York: Anchor Books, Paragon House, 1979, 1990), p. 233.
55. Ibid., p. 231.
56. Joseph Campbell, *Myths to Live By* (New York: Bantam Books, Viking, 1972, 1973).
57. J. Silverman, "Shamans and Acute Schizophrenia" in *American Anthropologist*, Vol. 69, No. 1, Feb. 1967, p. 22.
58. Ibid., p. 23.
59. Lee Sannella, *The Kundalini Experience—Psychosis or Transcendence?* (Lower Lake, CA: Integral Publishing, 1976, 1987). This book was originally published as *Kundalini—Psychosis or Transcendence?* The new edition has been revised and updated.
60. *Myths to Live By*, p. 209.

61. J. W. Perry, "Reconstitutive Process in the Psychopathology of the Self" in *Annals of the New York Academy of Sciences*, Vol. 96, Article 3, Jan. 27, 1962, pp. 854, 865–866, 876.
62. *The Psychotic Process*, p. 335.

Chapter 6
1. Gene Kieffer, *The Evolution of Joseph Campbell and America* (Darien, CT: The Kundalini Research Foundation, Ltd., 1988), p. 20.
2. Joseph Campbell, *The Mythic Image* (Princeton, NJ: Princeton University Press, 1974, 1981), pp. 281, 283.
3. *The Evolution of Joseph Campbell and America*, p. 23.
4. *The Mythic Image*, p. 332.
5. Joseph Campbell, *The Inner Reaches of Outer Space* (New York: HarperCollins, Perennial, 1986, 1988), p. 73.
6. *The Gospel of Sri Ramakrishna*, translated by Swami Nikhilananda (New York: Ramakrishna-Vivekananda Center, 1942), pp. 829–830.
7. Ibid.
8. *The Inner Reaches of Outer Space*, p. 74.
9. Ibid., p. 74.
10. Ibid., p. 80.
11. *The Evolution of Joseph Campbell and America*, p. 21.
12. *The Inner Reaches of Outer Space*, p. 83.
13. *The Evolution of Joseph Campbell and America*, p. 22.
14. *The Inner Reaches of Outer Space*, p. 89.
15. *The Evolution of Joseph Campbell and America*, p. 22.

Chapter 7
1. E. F. Torrey, *Surviving Schizophrenia: A Family Manual* (New York: HarperCollins, Perennial Library, 1983, 1988), p. 18.

2. Marguerite Sechehaye, *Autobiography of a Schizophrenic Girl* (New York: Grune & Stratton, 1951), pp. 40–41.

3. M. Coate, *Beyond All Reason* (Philadelphia: J. B. Lippincott, 1965), p. 21.

4. J. Chapman and A. McGhie, "Disorders of Attention and Perception in Early Schizophrenia," *British Journal of Medical Psychology* 34 (1961), pp. 103–116.

5. Ibid., pp. 66–67.

6. J. Lang, "The Other Side of Hallucinations," *American Journal of Psychiatry* 94 (1938), pp. 1090–1097.

7. *Surviving Schizophrenia*, pp. 55–56.

8. Gopi Krishna, *Kundalini: The Evolutionary Energy in Man* (Boston: Shambhala, 1967, 1970), p. 52.

9. Ibid.

10. Hiroshi Motoyama, *Theories of the Chakras: Bridge to Higher Consciousness* (Wheaton, IL: Theosophical Publishing House, Quest, 1981), p. 243.

11. *Surviving Schizophrenia*, p. 59.

12. Ibid., p. xiii.

13. Ibid., p. 73.

14. Ibid., p. 131.

15. Ibid., p. 132.

16. Ibid.

17. Ibid., p. 208.

18. Ibid., pp. 137–138.

19. Thomas S. Szasz, *Insanity: The Idea and Its Consequences* (New York: John Wiley & Sons, 1987), p. x.

20. Ibid., pp. 71–72.

21. Peter R. Breggin, M.D., *Toxic Psychiatry* (New York: St. Martin's Press, 1991), p. 84.

22. Ibid., p. 113.

23. Ibid.

24. Ibid.

25. Ibid.

26. Ibid.
27. *Surviving Schizophrenia*, p. 205.
28. Ibid., p. 44.
29. Parens patriae: the legal right to act as parent or guardian.
30. *Surviving Schizophrenia*, p. 328.
31. *Toxic Psychiatry*, p. 195.
32. Ibid., p. 47.
33. *Surviving Schizophrenia*, p. 189.
34. Ibid., p. 196.
35. Ibid., p. 245.
36. J. W. Perry, "Reconstitutive Process in the Psychopathology of the Self" in *Annals of the New York Academy of Sciences*, Vol. 96, Article 3, Jan. 27, 1962, p. 855.
37. Ibid., p. 875.
38. *Surviving Schizophrenia*, pp. 221–222.
39. R. E. Drake and L. I. Sederer, *Comprehensive Psychiatry* 2 (1986), pp. 313–326.
40. "Reconstitutive Process in the Psychopathology of the Self," pp. 873–874.
41. Joseph Campbell, *The Inner Reaches of Outer Space* (New York: HarperCollins, Perennial, 1986, 1988), p. 102.
42. *Spring: An Annual of Archetypal Psychology and Jungian Thought* (New York: Spring Publications, 1976), p. 1.
43. Sir John Woodroffe (Arthur Avalon), *The Serpent Power* (Madras, India: Ganesh & Co., Auromere, 1973).
44. *The Collected Works of C. G. Jung*, trans. R. F. C. Hull, Bollingen Series XX. Vol. 16: *The Practice of Psychotherapy* (Princeton, NJ: Princeton University Press, 1966), p. 335.
45. *Spring: An Annual of Archetypal Psychology and Jungian Thought* (New York: Spring Publications, 1975), p. 23.
46. Ibid., p. 26.
47. Ibid., p. 14.
48. *Spring: An Annual of Archetypal Psychology and Jungian Thought* (New York: Spring Publications, 1976), pp. 29–30.

Chapter 8

1. Gopi Krishna, *Kundalini—The Secret of Yoga* (Darien, CT: The Kundalini Research Foundation, Ltd.; and Toronto: F.I.N.D. Research, 1978), pp. 155–156.

2. Gopi Krishna, *The Awakening of Kundalini* (Bombay, India: D. B. Taraporevala, 1976), p. 4.

3. Ibid., p. 5.

4. Ibid.

5. Ibid., pp. 111–112.

6. Ibid., p. 112.

7. Gopi Krishna, *Kundalini: The Evolutionary Energy in Man* (Boston: Shambhala, 1967, 1970), p. 88.

8. Ibid., p. 90.

9. Charles Wilhelm, ed. *The Secret of the Golden Flower* (New York: Causeway Books, 1974), p. xi.

10. Ibid., p. 35.

11. Gene Kieffer, *The Secret of Kundalini* (Darien, CT: The Kundalini Research Foundation, Ltd., 1987), p. 27.

12. *The Awakening of Kundalini*, pp. 112–113.

13. See p. 189. From the Kundalini Research Foundation Ltd. files.

14. *The Secret of Kundalini*, p. 19.

15. *The Awakening of Kundalini*, p. 116.

16. Ibid.

17. Gopi Krishna, *The Way to Self-Knowledge* (Darien, CT: The Kundalini Research Foundation, Ltd., 1985).

18. *Kundalini—The Secret of Yoga*, p. 178.

19. Ibid., p. 177.

20. Ibid.

21. Stanislav Grof and Christina Grof, *The Stormy Search for the Self: A Guide to Personal Growth through Transformational Crisis* (Los Angeles: Jeremy P. Tarcher, 1990), p. 10.

22. *Kundalini—The Secret of Yoga*, p. 163.

23. Ibid.

24. Ibid., p. 175.

25. Ibid.
26. Ibid.

Chapter 9
1. Joseph Campbell, *Myths to Live By* (New York: Bantam Books, Viking, 1972), p. 215.
2. Ibid., pp. 215–216.

Epilogue
1. A. Theresa, *The Interior Castle* (New York: Paulist Press, The Washington Province of Discalced Carmelites, 1979), p. 123.
2. Ibid., p. 134.
3. St. John of the Cross, *Ascent of Mount Carmel*, edited and translated by E. Allison Peers (Garden City, NY: Doubleday & Company, Inc., 1958), p. 12.
4. Ibid., p. 78.
5. Ibid.
6. Lee Sannella, *Kundalini—Psychosis or Transcendence?* (San Francisco: H. S. Dakin, 1976; revised edition titled *The Kundalini Experience—Psychosis or Transcendence?* published by Integral Publishing, Lower Lake, CA, 1987).
7. R. Katz, "Education for Transcendence: Lessons from the !Kung Zhu Twasi," in *Journal of Transpersonal Psychology*, November 2, 1973.
8. *Kundalini—Psychosis or Transcendence?*, p. 14.
9. "Education for Transcendence: Lessons from the !Kung Zhu Twasi," (p. 14 in *Kundalini—Psychosis or Transcendence?*).
10. *Kundalini—Psychosis or Transcendance?*, p. 14.
11. Ibid., p. 15.
12. Ibid.
13. Ibid.
14. Ibid.

15. Gopi Krishna, *Kundalini—The Secret of Yoga* (Darien, CT: The Kundalini Research Foundation, Ltd.; and F.I.N.D. Research, 1978), p. 177.

16. Gopi Krishna, *Kundalini: The Evolutionary Energy in Man* (Boston: Shambhala, 1967, 1970), p. 89.

17. See p. 51.

18. John White, ed. *Kundalini: Evolution & Enlightenment* (New York: Anchor Books, Paragon House, 1979, 1990), p. 223.

19. Gene Kieffer, *The Secret of Kundalini* (Darien, CT: The Kundalini Research Foundation, Ltd., 1987), pp. 16–17.

20. Richard M. Bucke, *Cosmic Consciousness* (London: Innes & Sons, 1901; Reprint: Secaucus, NJ: Citadel Press, University Books, 1989), pp. 7–8.

21. *Kundalini: The Evolutionary Energy in Man*, p. 66.

22. See p. 42.

23. See p. 54.

24. See p. 203.

25. Mary Lutyens, *Krishnamurti: The Years of Fulfillment* (New York: Avon Books, 1975), p. 237.

26. *Cosmic Consciousness*, p. 186.

27. J. Kaplan, *Walt Whitman: A Life* (New York: Simon & Schuster, 1980), pp. 37–38.

28. *Cosmic Consciousness*, p. 188.

29. Walt Whitman, *Leaves of Grass* (New York: Modern Library), pp. 27–28.

30. *The Secret of Kundalini*, p. 10.